SMALL *Oxford* BOOKS

SNOBS

SMALL *Oxford* BOOKS

————————— ❧ —————————

SNOBS

————————— ❧ —————————

Compiled by
JASPER GRIFFIN

Oxford New York Toronto Melbourne
OXFORD UNIVERSITY PRESS
1982

Oxford University Press, Walton Street, Oxford OX2 6DP

London Glasgow New York Toronto
Delhi Bombay Calcutta Madras Karachi
Kuala Lumpur Singapore Hong Kong Tokyo
Nairobi Dar es Salaam Cape Town
Melbourne Auckland

and associates in
Beirut Berlin Ibadan Mexico City Nicosia

Compilation, introduction and editorial matter
© Jasper Griffin 1982

British Library Cataloguing in Publication Data

Griffin, Jasper
Snobs. — (Small Oxford books)
1. Snobs and snobbishness
I. Title
302 BJ1535.S7
ISBN 0-19-214128-7

Set by Western Printing Services Ltd.
Printed in Great Britain by
Hazell Watson & Viney Limited
Aylesbury, Bucks

Introduction

The appeal of the snobbish is one to which every bosom returns an echo. The more or less ignoble or absurd veneration of other people for what they think above them, whether socially, intellectually, or even morally, has been a mainstay of the mirth of mankind. It has also on occasion been tragic. The philosophical student of snobbishness finds himself, at moments, wondering how far this motive, potent but unavowed, can be wholly separated from any kind of progress or excellence. The adolescent who is anxious to admire Bach or Wordsworth because he knows that people whom he admires admire them, is on the normal road to real appreciation. Universities grow great as their reputation begins to attract the able and the aspiring. The use of forks at table seemed to our Tudor ancestors the height of affectation, and the first to follow that Italian custom doubtless did so, in large part, to impress their neighbours with their sophistication. Those who commissioned the works of art which we admire acted, perhaps more often than not, from motives among which the desire to excel the Joneses, or the Rossis, or the Duparcs, was by no means the least. Evolution itself is a process of rising above one's origins and one's station; when the first living creature left the primeval water to better itself on land, the world saw the first parvenu, and saw that it was good. The history of religion, too, is a rich reserve for the connoisseur of the snob. It is a rare saint who can resist making the claim to be the first and greatest of sinners, and settle, even in self-abasement, for a place among the middle class of Hell.

The historian of snobbishness is tempted to pass off his own work as something grander than it is; the quality is contagious. But this anthology does not really aim to be more than an amusing illustration of some of the varieties of the inexhaustible subject, in life and literature. I make no apology for mixing the real with the imagined; Aristotle tells us that poetry is more philosophical than history, and he might have added that anecdotes were no less instructive than annals, nor fiction than fact.

Macaulay liked to say, before producing some dazzling display of erudition, 'We have made no curious researches'. That claim can, with greater truth, be repeated here. A few of my specimens were hunted out, because some particular person had a claim to be included; malice may be detected, but not, I hope, injustice. I regret my failure to track down a couple of examples. Years ago I was familiar with a Victorian engraving of a little girl, sumptuously dressed and wearing a fur muff, holding out a coin to a crossing-sweeper with the words 'Here, poor boy without a hat, take this halfpenny'. Later I read in the *New Statesman* a sentence to this effect: 'In the 1880s many people found the spectacle of judges and peers capering about the stage and singing comic songs very funny; but nowadays some of us like to think we have got beyond that.' These two choice samples of my subject have not come to hand for the present work. But the field is so vast that no book can do more than cull a few blooms from it; *Snobs of All Ages*, if it were ever written, would be a book of unimaginable bulk. For we all feel, in an obscure but urgent way, that we are really grander than we seem, better than other people, more important than we can quite explain. Born kings and queens, but finding ourselves condemned to exile and insignificance, we snatch at such means as we can find to assert our rank, social, intellectual, or moral; and so we fall into snobbishness. James Boswell, most open of men, speaks for all mankind when he makes in his Journal the touching confession: 'As I have a good share of pride, which I think is proper and even noble, I am hurt with the taunts of ridicule and am unsatisfied if I do not feel myself something of a superior animal. This has always been my favourite idea in my best moments. Indeed, I have been obliged to deviate from it by a variety of circumstances . . .'

I conclude this Introduction with a dedication. This book should be inscribed to a great hero of its subject. I have found no greater example of the snob than the nameless French gentleman of whom Chamfort tells us: 'A fanatical social climber, observing that all round the Palace of Versailles it stank of urine, told his own tenants and servants to come and make water round his château.' To his aspiring shade, and to other heroic snobs like him, this book is dedicated.

It is Beautiful to study even the Snobbish; to trace Snobs through history.

W. M. Thackeray, Preface to *The Book of Snobs*, 1847

Because there's snobbery in every age.

W. H. Auden, *Letter to Lord Byron*, 1937

I would have given a good deal to have been born an aristocrat.

D. H. Lawrence, letter to Lady Ottoline Morrell

♔

He that Writes one Book out of an *Hundred* may be rather said to be a Collector, than an Author; and flourishes like *Covent-Garden-Market*, with *Fruit* not growing but withering upon his hands.

Tom Brown, *Laconics*, 1701

Aristocratic Snobs

A HANDFUL OF DUKES

Both as snobs and as connoisseurs of snobbishness we take pleasure in the society of Dukes; and no Duke has ever been more satisfyingly ducal than the Duke of Dorset, that sublime man, in Zuleika Dobson.

A few minutes before half-past seven, the Duke, arrayed for dinner, passed leisurely up the High. The arresting feature of his costume was a mulberry-coloured coat, with brass buttons. This, to anyone versed in Oxford lore, betokened him a member of the Junta. It is awful to think that a casual stranger might have mistaken him for a footman. It does not do to think of such things.

The tradesmen, at the doors of their shops, bowed low as he passed, rubbing their hands and smiling, hoping inwardly that they took no liberty in sharing the cool rosy air of the evening with his Grace. They noted that he wore in his shirt-front a black pearl and a pink. 'Daring, but becoming,' they opined.

The rooms of the Junta were over a stationer's shop, next door but one to the Mitre. They were small rooms; but as the Junta had now, besides the Duke, only two members, and as no member might introduce more than one guest, there was ample space.

The Duke had been elected in his second term. At that time there were four members; but these were all leaving Oxford at the end of the summer term, and there seemed to be in the ranks of the Bullingdon and the Loder no one quite eligible for the Junta, that holy of holies. Thus it was that the Duke inaugurated in solitude his second year of membership. From time to time, he proposed and seconded a few candidates, after 'sounding' them as to whether they were willing to join. But always, when election evening – the last Tuesday of term – drew near, he began to have his doubts about these fellows. This one was 'rowdy'; that one was over-dressed; another did not ride quite straight to hounds; in the pedigree of another a bar-sinister was more than suspected. Election evening was always a rather melan-choly time. After dinner, when the two club servants had placed on the mahogany the time-worn Candidates' Book and the ballot-box, and had noiselessly with-drawn, the Duke, clearing his throat, read aloud to himself 'Mr So-and-So, of Such-and-Such College, proposed by the Duke of Dorset, seconded by the Duke of Dorset,' and, in every case, when he drew out the drawer of the ballot-box, found it was a black ball that he had dropped into the urn. Thus it was that at the end of the summer term the annual photographic 'group' taken by Messrs. Hills and Saunders was a present-ment of the Duke alone.

In the course of his third year he had become less exclusive. Not because there seemed to be anyone really worthy of the Junta; but because the Junta, having thriven since the eighteenth century, must not die. Suppose – one never knew – he were struck by lightning, the Junta would be no more. So, not without reluctance, but unanimously, he had elected The MacQuern, of Balliol, and Sir John Marraby, of Brasenose.

Max Beerbohm, *Zuleika Dobson*, 1911

Less amusing was the Sixth Duke of Somerset, called the Proud Duke (1662–1748), of whom it is told that

on one occasion his second wife tapped him lightly with her fan. 'Madam', he said imperiously, 'my first

Duchess was a Percy, and she never took such a liberty.'

He tried to avoid ever being seen by those of lower status, built houses at strategic points between Petworth and London to ensure that he need never stay at an inn, and sent couriers before him to clear the roads for his passage. It comes as a relief to read that 'one man responded ... by thrusting a pig in the Duke's face'.

Elevation to a dukedom changed the manners of James Bridges, first Duke of Chandos; the resentful Swift, not a man to be snubbed with impunity, wrote:

James Bridges and the Dean had long been friends;
James is be-duked, of course their friendship ends.
But sure the Dean deserves a sharp rebuke,
From knowing James, to boast he knows the Duke.

From fact to fiction. That intemperate old buffer, Alaric, Duke of Dunstable, is in characteristic form in P. G. Wodehouse's Uncle Fred in the Spring-time; *his nephew Ricky, a poet, is trying to touch him for £250 to buy an onion soup bar, with the further intention of marrying.*

'I want to get married,' he said.

If the Duke's heart was touched, his rugged exterior showed no sign of it. His eyes came out of his head like a prawn's, and once more his moustache foamed up against his breakwater of a nose.

'Married?' he cried. 'What do you mean, married? Don't be an ass.'

Ricky had started the day with a tenderness towards all created things, and this attitude he had hoped to be able to maintain. But he could not help feeling that Providence, in creating his Uncle Alaric, was trying him a little high.

'I never heard such nonsense in my life. How the

devil can you afford to get married? You've got about twopence a year which your mother left you, and I don't suppose you make enough out of those sonnets of yours to keep you in cigarettes.'

'That's why I meant to buy this onion soup bar.'

'And a nice fool you would look, selling onion soup.'

With a strong effort, Ricky succeeded in making no comment on this. It seemed to him that silence was best. Galling though it was to allow his companion to score debating points, it was better than to close all avenues leading to an appeasement with a blistering repartee. At the moment, moreover, he could not think of a blistering repartee.

The Duke's moustache was rising and falling like seaweed on an ebb tide.

'And a nice fool I'd look, going about trying to explain away a nephew who dished soup out of a tureen. It's been bad enough having to tell my friends you write poetry. "What's that nephew of yours doing these days?" ' the Duke proceeded, giving an imitation of an enquiring friend with – for some reason – a falsetto voice. ' "The Guards? Diplomatic Service? Reading for the Bar?" "No," I tell them. "He's writing poetry," and there's an awkward silence. And now you want me to have to spread it about that you've become a blasted soup-dispenser. Gah!'

A deep flush had spread itself over Ricky's face. His temper, always a little inclined to be up and doing, had begun to flex its muscles like an acrobat about to do a trick.

'As for this idea of yours of getting married . . . Why do you want to get married? Hey? Why?'

'Oh, just to score off the girl. I dislike her.'

'What!'

'Why do you think I want to get married? Why do people usually want to get married? I want to get married because I've found the most wonderful girl in the world, and I love her.'

'You said you disliked her.'

'I was merely trying to be funny.'

The Duke took in a mouthful of moustache, chewed it for a moment, seemed dissatisfied with the flavour, and expelled it again with another forceful puff.

'Who is she?'

'Nobody you know.'

'Well, who's her father?'

'Oh, nobody special.'

A sudden, sinister calm fell upon the Duke, causing his manner to resemble that of a volcano which is holding itself in by sheer will-power.

'You don't need to tell me any more. I see it all. The wench is a dashed outsider.'

'She is not!'

'Don't argue with me . . . she's obviously the scum of the earth. The way a man's nephews get entangled with the dregs of the human species is enough to give one apoplexy. I absolutely forbid you to marry this female crossing-sweeper.'

The sort of girl of whom the Duke of Dunstable might have approved is shown in a sketch from The Gate Revue *of 1938, by Diana Morgan.*

KENSINGTON GIRLS

Pont Street on a summer morning in the Thirties
Three nice girls come forward and sing:

> We're Kensington Girls from Kensington
>> Gore
> Honest and decent and clean to the core,
> Hoping to marry as soon as we can
> Just for saving the race and for saving a
>> man!

Cora   My name is Cora, my father's a Captain,
       My mother's first cousin's a Lord;
       I've just been presented, I thought it was
           heaven,
       But I had to pretend I was bored.
       I worship my dog and tho' usually mild
       Cruelty to animals just drives me wild,
       It's so much more sporting to be cruel to
           a child.

All   Girls of Kensington Gore.

Nora   My name is Nora, my father's a Major,
       I've got a young man in a ship;
       He's rolling in money with two lovely
           cars,
       So I hope he won't give me the slip.
       I go to Miss Fogerty's school every day,
       They teach me to act in a nice refined way,
       I couldn't face Rep. but the West End's
           O.K.

All   Girls of Kensington Gore!

Belinda   My name's Belinda, my father's a General
Though he never went to the front;
I'm socially better than these other two,
For you see in the winter I hunt.
I love cocktail parties and things of that
      sort,
I'm afraid I'm about rather more than I
      ought,
But I still tell young men I just live for
      my sport,

All   Girls of Kensington Gore:

O, ye of lesser breed
Listen to our creed!

There is one place in which to live and
      that is Kensington
(Including parts of Chelsea and at
      Brompton Square).
There is one uniform to wear
A good fur coat
A string of pearls
And a black dress
For English Girls.
There is one shop and that is Harrods where
We've lots of time to stand and stare.
There are no plays but those that run a
      hundred nights
And have lots of names in lights.
There are no men
Excepting those in the Buffs, the Blues,
      and the H.A.C.
Those are the ones for me.
(He He He He He He!)
We are the backbone of the country,
The really nice girls
Of quite good family

Who get married about twenty-four,
Who go to India,
South Africa,
And Burma,
That's what God made us for!

We're Kensington Girls from Kensington
  Gore
Not very rich and not very poor!
Hoping to marry as soon as we can
For the sake of the race – and the sake of
  a man!

YONDER PEASANT, WHO IS HE?

We leave even Dukes beneath us with a passage of Proust, the greatest, perhaps, of all analysts of snobbishness, describing the Princess of Parma; here pride and humility embrace each other in such a way that even the loving Proustian scalpel cannot separate them.

Her amiability sprang from two causes. The first and more general was the upbringing which this daughter of kings had received. Her mother (not merely related to all the royal families of Europe but furthermore – in contrast to the ducal house of Parma – richer than any reigning princess) had instilled into her from her earliest childhood the arrogantly humble precepts of an evangelical snobbery; and to-day every line of the daughter's face, the curve of her shoulders, the movements of her arms, seemed to repeat the lesson: 'Remember that if God has caused you to be born on the steps of a throne you ought not to make that a reason for looking down upon those to whom Divine Providence has willed (wherefore His Name be praised) that you should be superior by birth and fortune. On the contrary, you must be kind to the lowly. Your ancestors were Princes of Cleves and Juliers from the year 647; God in His bounty has decreed that you should hold practically all the shares in the Suez Canal and three times as many Royal Dutch as Edmond de Rothschild; your pedigree in a direct line has been established by genealogists from the year 63 of the Christian era; you have as sisters-in-law two empresses. Therefore never seem in your speech to be recalling these great privileges, not that they are precarious (for nothing can alter the antiquity of blood, while the world will always need oil), but because it is unnecessary to point out that you are better born than other people or that your investments are all gilt-edged, since everyone knows these facts already. Be helpful to the needy. Give to all those whom the bounty of heaven has been graciously pleased to put beneath you as much as you can give them without forfeiting your rank, that is to say help in the form of money, even your personal service by their sickbeds, but of course never any invitations to your soirées, which would do them no possible good and, by diminishing your prestige, would reduce the efficacy of your benevolent activities.'

And so even at the moments when she could not do good the Princess endeavoured to shew, or rather to let it be thought, by all the external signs of dumb language, that she did not consider herself superior to the people among whom she found herself thrown.

Marcel Proust, *Remembrance of Things Past*,
trans. C. K. Scott Moncrieff and Terence Kilmartin, 1980

In reality, great persons were not always so agreeable. Chamfort tells us of the 'excessive and ridiculous vanity' of Le Tellier-Louvois, Archbishop of Rheims; it is a nice point that the victim is a Duke.

On one occasion the Duke of A . . . , who had been away from the Court for years, was coming back to

Versailles from Berri, where he was Governor of the province. His carriage was overturned and damaged. It was bitterly cold; he was told that to repair it would take two hours. He saw an outrider, and asked to whom he belonged; the answer was that he belonged to the Archbishop of Rheims, who was also going to Versailles. He sent his attendants away, keeping only one and telling him not to show himself without his orders. The Archbishop came up. The Duke told one of the Archbishop's men to ask for a seat for a gentleman, whose carriage was damaged, and who would have to wait two hours for it to be repaired. The servant did as he was told. 'What sort of man is he?' said the Archbishop. 'Is he someone of good manners?' 'I think so, Monseigneur; his air is distinguished.' 'What do you mean by distinguished? Is he well dressed?' 'Simply, Monseigneur, but well.' 'Has he servants?' 'I think so, Monseigneur.' 'Go and find out.' (The servant goes and comes back). 'Monseigneur, he has sent them on to Versailles.' 'Ah! That is something – but not everything. Ask him if he is a gentleman.' (The servant goes and comes back). 'Yes, Monseigneur, he is a gentleman.' 'Well, it's time for him to come here; we'll see what he is.' The Duke appears and greets him. The Archbishop nods, and moves to leave a very small space in his coach. He sees the cross of the Order of St. Louis. 'Monsieur,' he says, 'I am sorry to have kept you waiting, – but you will understand that I could not give a seat in my coach to a nobody. I know you are a gentleman. You have done some service, I see!' 'Yes, Monseigneur.' 'And you are on your way to Versailles?' 'Yes, Monseigneur.' 'To the offices, I suppose?' 'No; I am not involved with the offices. I am on my way to give thanks . . . ' 'To whom? To M. de Louvois?' 'No, Monseigneur, to the King.' 'The King!' (Here the Archbishop moves up and leaves a little more room). 'The King has conferred some favour on you recently?' 'No, Monseigneur, it is a long story.' 'Tell me.' 'Some years ago my daughter married a man of only moderate means' (the Archbishop takes back some of the room he had left) 'but of a great name' (the Archbishop recedes again). The Duke goes on: 'His Majesty kindly interested himself in this marriage' (the Archbishop leaves a large space) 'and had promised my son-in-law the first vacancy that came up' – 'As what? Some minor governorship, I assume. Of what town?' 'It's not a governorship of a town, Monseigneur, but of a province.' 'Of a province!' cries the Archbishop, squeezing back into the corner. 'Yes, and now he is to have one which has fallen vacant.' 'Which one?' 'Mine, the governorship of Berri, which I wish to hand over to my son-in-law.' 'What! Monsieur, so you are . . . you are the Duke of . . . ' (he makes to get out of the coach). 'But, Monsieur le Duc, why did you not tell me? It's unbelievable! What a position you put me in! Forgive me for making you wait . . . My idiot servant did not tell me . . . It's a good thing I took your word that you were a gentleman – so many people say they are when they aren't! M. le Duc, I am overwhelmed.' 'Monseigneur, seat yourself again. Forgive your servant, who told you only that I was a gentleman, and exposed you to the risk of allowing into your coach an old soldier without a title; and forgive me too, for not beginning by proving my claim to enter your carriage.'

Chamfort (1741–94), *Maximes, caractères et anecdotes*

👑

Sir Osbert Sitwell describes his father gazing wistfully out over one of the most thickly peopled areas of England and saying 'Of course, there's absolutely no one between us and the Locker-Lampsons'.

He would have been at home with Jane Austen's

baronet in Persuasion (*1818*), *whose idea of a gentleman was, as we shall see, exclusive. Sir Walter Elliot's agent is working to induce him to let his house to Admiral Croft, and thinks to advance his cause by mentioning his wife's connections:*

. . . 'And moreover, Sir Walter, I found she was not quite unconnected in this country, any more than her husband; that is to say, she is sister to a gentleman who did live amongst us once; she told me so herself: sister to the gentleman who lived a few years back, at Monkford. Bless me! what was his name? At this moment I cannot recollect his name, though I have heard it so lately. Penelope, my dear, can you help me to the name of the gentleman who lived at Monkford – Mrs Croft's brother?'

But Mrs Clay was talking so eagerly with Miss Elliot, that she did not hear the appeal.

'I have no conception whom you can mean, Shepherd; I remember no gentleman resident at Monkford since the time of old Governor Trent.'

'Bless me! how very odd! I shall forget my own name soon, I suppose. A name that I am so very well acquainted with; knew the gentleman so well by sight; seen him a hundred times; came to consult me once, I remember, about a trespass of one of his neighbours; farmer's man breaking into his orchard – wall torn down – apples stolen – caught in the fact; and afterwards, contrary to my judgment, submitted to an amicable compromise. Very odd indeed!'

After waiting another moment –

'You mean Mr Wentworth, I suppose,' said Anne.

Mr Shepherd was all gratitude.

'Wentworth was the very name! Mr Wentworth was the very man. He had the curacy of Monkford, you know, Sir Walter, some time back for two or three years. Came there about the year —5, I take it. You remember him, I am sure.'

'Wentworth? Oh! ay, – Mr Wentworth, the curate of Monkford. You misled me by the term *gentleman*. I thought you were speaking of some man of property: Mr Wentworth was nobody, I remember; quite un-connected; nothing to do with the Strafford family. One wonders how the names of many of our nobility become so common.'

As Mr Shepherd perceived that this connexion of the Crofts did them no service with Sir Walter, he mentioned it no more . . .

BLUE BLOOD

A modern approach to titles, appropriate to an age more nervous about its reverence, comes out in a poem by Justin Richardson:

TITLES

Come, let us be frank –

We are all, or nearly all, attracted by rank.

Of *course* we're not snobs, of *course* we don't bow
    and scrape

Or alter our standards in any degree or shape –

What's in a handle? What come to that's in a name?

All the same –

It's nice, other things being equal, to write 'Dear
    Sir Hugh';

'Dear Hodgkins' somehow is markedly less exciting.

'Lord Privilege phoned; will you meet him at twenty
    to . . . '

More sort of *inviting*.

The added respect that we get from reflected glory

Appeals to the part of our Socialist souls that's
    Tory.

[13]

And, though it's a thing that none of us might
    confess,
When we do meet a title we either employ it *less*
Or *more* than we normally would –
Not that that proves us snobs, that's *well*
    understood.
We are playing charades, we are making the tinsel
    glitter;
If we knew it, escaping the sink and the baby-sitter.
'Lady Jane!' – there's a grain of snuff on our
    ruffled wrist.
'Sir John!' – and our long white fingers are lightly
    kissed.

Punch, 11 April 1951

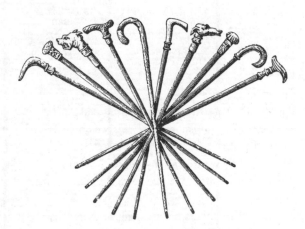

'*Chips' Channon wrote of Ramsay Macdonald,*

He never smiles except when he is talking to an elder
son, although he was once very pleasant to me, on the
day that our last Royal dinner party was described in
the Press.

Chips, the Diaries of Sir H. Channon,
ed. R. R. James, 1967

[14]

David Copperfield, in his wide-eyed progress through the world, came up against this sort of thing in a more grotesque and terrific form:

. . . The dinner was very long, and the conversation was about the Aristocracy – and Blood. Mrs Waterbrook repeatedly told us that, if she had a weakness, it was Blood . . .

We might have been a party of Ogres, the conversation assumed such a sanguine complexion.

'I confess I am of Mrs Waterbrook's opinion,' said Mr Waterbrook, with his wine-glass at his eye. 'Other things are all very well in their way, but give me Blood!'

'Oh! There is nothing,' observed Hamlet's aunt, 'so satisfactory to one! There is nothing that is so much one's *beau idéal* of – of all that sort of thing, speaking generally. There are some low minds (not many, I am happy to believe, but there are *some*) that would prefer to do what *I* should call bow down before idols. Positively Idols! Before services, intellect, and so on. But these are intangible points. Blood is not so. We see Blood in a nose, and we know it. We meet with it in a chin, and we say, "There it is! That's Blood!" It is an actual matter of fact. We point it out. It admits of no doubt.'

The simpering fellow with the weak legs, who had taken Agnes down, stated the question more decisively yet, I thought.

'Oh, you know, deuce take it,' said this gentleman, looking round the board with an imbecile smile, 'we can't forego Blood, you know. We must have Blood, you know. Some young fellows, you know, may be a little behind their station, perhaps, in point of education and behaviour, and may go a little wrong, you know, and get themselves and other people into a variety of fixes – and all that – but deuce take it, it's delightful to reflect that they've got Blood in 'em!

Myself, I'd rather at any time be knocked down by a
man who had got Blood in him than I'd be picked up
by a man who hadn't!'

Charles Dickens, *David Copperfield*, 1850

*Thackeray gives us a classic English snob in old Mr
Osborne, the wealthy merchant of* Vanity Fair (*1848*).
*Here he is revelling in the high company kept by his son,
an officer in an expensive regiment.*

'A pretty boy, indeed. Haven't I heard of your
doings, sir, with Lord Tarquin, Captain Crawley of
the Guards, the Honourable Mr Deuceace, and that
set. Have a care, sir, have a care.'

The old gentleman pronounced these aristocratic
names with the greatest gusto. Whenever he met a great
man he grovelled before him, and my-lorded him
as only a free-born Briton can do. He came home and
looked out his history in the Peerage: he introduced
his name into his daily conversation; he bragged about
his lordship to his daughters. He fell down prostrate
and basked in him as a Neapolitan beggar does in the
sun. George was alarmed when he heard the names.
He feared his father might have been informed of
certain transactions at play. But the old moralist eased
him by saying serenely:—

'Well, well, young men will be young men. And the
comfort to me is, George, that living in the best society
in England, as I hope you do; as I think you do; as
my means will allow you to do – '

'Thank you, sir,' says George, making his point at
once. 'One can't live with these great folks for nothing;
and my purse, sir, look at it;' and he held up a little
token which had been netted by Amelia, and contained
the very last of Dobbin's pound notes.

'You shan't want, sir. The British merchant's son
shan't want, sir. My guineas are as good as theirs,

George, my boy; and I don't grudge 'em. Call on
Mr Chopper as you go through the City tomorrow;
he'll have something for you. I don't grudge money
when I know you're in good society, because I know
that good society can never go wrong. There's no pride
in me. I was a humbly born man – but you have had
advantages. Make a good use of 'em. Mix with the
young nobility. There's many of 'em who can't spend
a dollar to your guinea, my boy.'

GREAT LADIES

*The unbending code of the aristocrat emerges in a comical
light when we hear the Princesse de Lieven, for years one
of the most formidable ladies in the society of London and
Paris, give her answer to the question whether, after her
husband's death, she would now marry Guizot, the utterly
middle-class politician and historian with whom she had
been living for several years, and with whom she continued
to live until her death. 'Oh! my dear', she replied, 'can
you see me being announced as Mrs Guizot?'*

♛

*Being a great lady was, in the highest reaches, a highly
skilled business. Nothing was more important than the
exactness with which she judged her address to different
people. Hippolyte Taine, the historian of the* ancien
régime, *observed that a great lady could receive ten
persons with one courtesy, bestowing on each, through a
movement of her head or by a glance, all that he was
entitled to from position, standing, and birth.*

She was never mistaken, and never hesitated in these
subtle distinctions; with incomparable tact, dexterity,
and flexibility of tone, she regulated the degrees of her
welcome. She had one for women of condition, one for
women of quality, one for women of the court, one for

titled women, one for women of historic names, another for women of high birth personally, but married to men beneath them; another for women who by marriage have changed a common into a distinguished name; another still for women of reputable names in the law; and, finally, another for those whose distinction consists chiefly of expensive houses and good suppers. A stranger would be amazed on seeing with what certain and adroit steps she circulated among so many watchful vanities without ever giving or receiving a check. She knew how to express it all through the style of her salutations; a varied style, extending through imperceptible gradations, from the accessory of a single shrug of the shoulder, almost an impertinence, to that noble and deferential reverence which so few women, even of the court, know how to do well; that slow bending forward, with lowered eyes and straightened figure, gradually recovering and modestly glancing at the person while gracefully raising the body up, altogether much more refined and more delicate than words, but very expressive as the means of manifesting respect.

H. Taine, *The Ancient Regime*, 1878,
trans. J. Durand

On a humbler level we find the same thing in Scotland:

Mrs Helen Carnegy of Craigo was a thorough specimen of this class of old Scottish ladies. She lived in Montrose and died in 1818, at the advanced age of ninety-one. She was a Jacobite, and very aristocratic in her feelings, but on social terms with many burghers of Montrose, or Munross, as it was called. She preserved a very nice distinction of addresses, suited to different individuals in the town, according as she placed them in the scale of her consideration. She liked a party at quadrille, and sent out her servant every morning to invite the ladies required to make up the game, and her directions were graduated thus: 'Nelly, ye'll ging to Lady Carnegy's, and mak my compliments, and ask the *honour* of her ladyship's company, and that of the Miss Carnegies, to tea this evening; and if they canna come, ging to the Miss Mudies, and ask the *pleasure* of their company; and if they canna come, ye may ging to Miss Hunter and ask the *favour* of her company; and if she canna come, ging to Lucky Spark and *bid her come.*'

G. B. Ramsay, *Reminiscences of Scottish Life and Character*, 1861

THE SNUB

Persons who did not belong in grand company courted annihilation if they entered it. The following passages are quoted from Hints on Etiquette and the Usages of Society, with a Glance at Bad Habits, *published anonymously in 1834:*

ADVICE TO TRADESPEOPLE

By tradespeople I do not mean merchants or manufacturers, but shopkeepers and retailers of various goods, who will do well to remember that people are respectable in their own sphere only, and that when they attempt to step out of it *they cease to be so.* When exceptions are made by the world, it is generally in favour of brilliant genius or extraordinary acquirement, and *even then*, it can only be by the prevailing suffrage of society; therefore do not attempt to claim the acquaintance of those above you, lest you meet a mortifying repulse. Many will say, 'We are just as good as they are, and as respectable'. SO YOU ARE, but yet not fit companions for each other. Society is divided into various orders, each class having its own views, its peculiar education, habits, and tastes . . .

So much for a general warning; now for a terrible example:

An unfortunate Clerk of the Treasury, who, because he was in the receipt of a good salary, and being also a 'triton among the minnows' of Clapham Common, fancied himself a great man, dined at the B—f S—k Club, where he sat next to a noble Duke, who, desirous of putting him at ease, conversed freely with him, yet probably forgot even the existence of such a person half an hour afterwards. Meeting his Grace in the street some days after, and encouraged by his previous condescension, the hero of the quill, bent on claiming his acquaintance, accosted him in a familiar 'hail-fellow-well-met-ish' manner – 'Ah, my Lord, how d'ye do?' The Duke looked surprised. 'May I know, Sir, *to whom* I have the honour of speaking?' said his Grace, drawing up. 'Oh! why – don't you know? We dined together at the B—f S—k Club, the other evening! – I'm MR TIMMS OF THE TREASURY!!' 'Then,' said the Duke, turning on his heel, 'MR TIMMS OF THE TREASURY, I wish you *a good morning*'.

A more feline snub, meant to be felt but not harsh enough for a protest, is preserved at the opening of a letter of Cicero to a banker named Volumnius, who had been just a little too familiar.

You were quite right to sign your letter to me simply

'Volumnius', like a close friend, without using your first name – but I did think at first that it was from Volumnius the Senator, with whom I am on close terms . . .

Cicero, Epistulae ad familiares 7.32, 51 BC

Proust gives us a noble example of the snub by the Baron de Charlus. M. Verdurin, his host, has shown his utter ignorance of high society by seating the Baron below the Marquis de Cambremer, who to Charlus is not really an aristocrat at all. In this complex passage M. Verdurin claims to be above that sort of distinction – a claim annihilated by the Baron's reply that he is, in reality, beneath it. Two sorts of snobbishness meet in collision.

M. Verdurin wanted to apologise for this to M. de Charlus . . . and to give him his reasons, chiefly for the pleasure of discussing these social distinctions with a man of title, momentarily the inferior of those who assigned to him the place to which they considered him entitled. But first of all he was anxious to make it clear to M. de Charlus that intellectually he esteemed him too highly to suppose that he could pay any attention to these trivialities.

'Forgive my mentioning these trifles', he began, 'for I can well imagine how little importance you attach to them. Middle-class minds take them seriously, but the others, the artists, the people who are really *of our sort*, don't give a rap for them . . . '

'What were you going to say to me?' interrupted M. de Charlus . . .

'Only that we put you on the left', replied M. Verdurin.

M. de Charlus, with a tolerant, genial, insolent smile, replied: 'Why, that's not of the slightest importance, *here*!' And he gave a little laugh that was all his own – a laugh that came to him probably from some Bavarian or Lorraine grandmother, who herself had inherited it, in identical form, from an ancestress, so that it had tinkled now, unchanged, for a good many centuries in little old-fashioned European courts, and one could appreciate its precious quality, like that of certain old musical instruments that have become very rare . . .

'But,' explained M. Verdurin, hurt, 'we did it on purpose. I attach no importance whatever to titles of nobility,' he went on, with that contemptuous smile which I have seen so many people assume when they speak of something they do not possess to those who will thereby, they imagine, be prevented from using it to show their superiority over them. 'But you see, since we happened to have M. de Cambremer here, and he's a marquis, while you're only a baron . . .'

'Pardon me,' M. de Charlus haughtily replied to the astonished Verdurin, 'I am also Duke of Brabant, Squire of Montargis, Prince of Oléron, of Carency, of Viareggio and of the Dunes. However, it's not of the slightest importance. Please don't distress yourself,' he concluded, resuming his delicate smile which blossomed at these final words: 'I could see at a glance you were out of your depth.'

Marcel Proust, *Remembrance of Things Past*,
trans. C. K. Scott Moncrieff and Terence Kilmartin, 1980

GREAT ASPIRATIONS

Dean Swift found a characteristically barbed way of hitting off the love of grand society, saying 'I love good creditable acquaintance; I love to be the worst of the company'.

♛

No collection of snobs would be complete without Hilaire Belloc's Godolphin Horne, true brother of the great

historic snobs, but unlucky enough to have his being in a
Cautionary Tale, *where retribution follows pride with a*
punctuality for which in real life we look in vain.

GODOLPHIN HORNE, WHO WAS CURSED WITH THE SIN OF PRIDE AND BECAME A BOOT-BLACK

Godolphin Horne was Nobly Born;
He held the Human Race in scorn,
And lived with all his Sisters where
His father lived, in Berkeley Square.
And oh! the lad was Deathly Proud!
He never shook your Hand or Bowed,
But merely smirked and nodded thus:
How perfectly ridiculous!
Alas! that such Affected Tricks
Should flourish in a Child of Six!
(For such was Young Godolphin's age).
Just then, the Court required a Page,
Whereat the Lord High Chamberlain
(The kindest and the Best of Men),
He went good-naturedly and took
A Perfectly Enormous Book
Called *People Qualified to Be*
Attendant on His Majesty,
And murmured, as he scanned the list
(To see that no one should be missed),
'There's William Coutts has got the Flue,
And Billy Higgs would never do,
And Guy de Vere is far too young,
And . . . wasn't D'Alton's Father hung?
And as for Alexander Byng! – . . .
I think I know the kind of thing,
A Churchman, cleanly, nobly born,
Come: let us say Godolphin Horne?'
But hardly had he said the word
When Murmurs of Dissent were heard.

The King of Iceland's Eldest Son
Said, 'Thank you! I am taking none!'
The Aged Duchess of Athlone
Remarked, in her sub-acid tone,
'I doubt if He is what we need!'
With which the Bishops all agreed;
And even Lady Mary Flood,
(So kind, and oh! so *really* good),
Said 'No! He wouldn't do at all,
He'd make us feel a lot too small'.
The Chamberlain said, ' . . . Well, well, well!
No doubt you're right . . . one cannot tell!'
He took his Gold and Diamond Pen
And Scratched Godolphin out again.
So now Godolphin is the Boy
Who blacks the Boots at the Savoy.

Hilaire Belloc, *Cautionary Tales for Children*, 1907

A little luckier than Godolphin as a courtier was James Boswell, who as he tells us in his Journal was kindly received by a Prince:

And now let me record my talents as a courtier. From my earliest years I have respected the great. In the groves of Auchinleck I have indulged pleasing hopes of ambition . . . The Prince of Baden-Durlach has an order to give. He creates Knights of the Order of Fidelity. They wear a star and a ribbon hanging from their necks. My Lord Wemyss has this order. I fixed my inclination upon it. I was determined if possible to obtain it. When the Prince honoured me so far as to grant me his correspondence, I thought he would surely grant me his order. I asked him once *en passant* if only counts could have it. He said, 'It is enough to be a good gentleman.' Munzesheim had told me that the Prince was a little nice in giving it. This being my last day here, I was presented to take leave. The Prince said, 'I cannot ask you to stay longer, as I am afraid you would tire.' I said, by no means, but I was a little hurried at present, and would return again and pass a longer time. I then took courage and said, 'Sir, I have a favour to ask of you, a very great favour. I don't know whether I should mention it.' I was quite the courtier, for I appeared modest and embarrassed, when in reality I was perfectly unconcerned. He said, 'What, Sir?' I replied, 'Your Highness told me that a good gentleman might have your Highness's order. Sir, might I presume to ask you that, if I bring you proof of my being a very good gentleman, I may obtain the order?' He paused. I looked at him steadily. He answered, 'I shall think of it.' I said, 'Sir, you have already been so good to me that I flatter myself that I have the merit for obtaining a favour. As to my rank, I can assure you that I am a very old gentleman' (some days ago I had given his Highness a history of my family) 'and it may sound strange, but, Sir, I can count kindred with my sovereign from my being related to the family of Lennox and the royal family of Stuart. Sir, I am one of your old proud Scots. If you grant me this favour, you will make me happy for life, in adding honour to my family; and I shall be proud to wear in my own country the Order of Fidelity of such a prince.' He seemed pleased. I said, 'I hope, Sir, you do not take amiss my having mentioned this. I was anxious to obtain it, and I thought it was pity to want what I valued so highly, for want of boldness to ask it.' He said, 'Let me have your genealogy attested, and when you return, we shall see.' Oh, I shall have it. I took leave of his Highness with much respect.

It is sad to have to record that Boswell did not get it.

Boswell might have got on well with Mr Salteena, the aspiring hero of The Young Visiters, *whom we find here taking the first steps towards being a gentleman.*

With a nervous bound Mr Salteena obeyed these directions and found himself in a small but handsome compartment done in dark green lether with crests on the chairs. Over the mantlepiece was hung the painting of a lady in a low neck looking quite the thing. By the desk was seated a tall man of 35 with very nice eyes of a twinkly nature and curly hair he wore a quite plain suit of palest grey but well made and on the table reposed a grey top hat which had evidently been on his head recently. He had a rose in his button hole also a signet ring.

Hullo said this plesant fellow as Mr Salteena was spell bound on mat.

Hullo your Lord Ship responded our hero bowing low and dropping his top hat do I adress the Earl of Clincham.

You do said the Earl with a homely smile and who do I adress eh.

Our hero bowed again Alfred Salteena he said in deep tones.

Oh I see said the kindly earl well come in my man and tell me who you are.

Mr Salteena seated himself gingerly on the edge of a crested chair.

To tell you the truth my Lord I am not anyone of import and I am not a gentleman as they say he ended getting very red and hot.

Have some whiskey said lord Clincham and he poured the liquid into a glass at his elbow. Mr Salteena lapped it up thankfully.

Well my man said the good natured earl what I say is what dose it matter we cant all be of the Blood royal can we.

No said Mr Salteena but I suppose you are.

Lord Clincham waved a careless hand. A small portion flows in my veins he said but it dose not worry me at all and after all he added piously at the Day of Judgement what will be the odds.

Mr Salteena heaved a sigh. I was thinking of this world he said.

Oh I see said the Earl but my own idear is that these things are as piffle before the wind.

Not being an earl I cant say answered our hero but may I beg you to read this letter my Lord. He produced Bernards note from his coat tails. The Earl of Clincham took it in his long fingers. . . .

Daisy Ashford (aged 9), *The Young Visiters*, 1919

Real life contained people hardly less comical in their aspirations than poor Mr Salteena. Rich Americans bought their way into Society; high personages were happy to be bought, while affecting to despise the parvenus. It is hard not to feel that the two parties were pretty equally matched; and that perhaps Henry James saw more nuances to the meeting of America and Europe than were always really present. Elsa Maxwell, the celebrated hostess, tells us in her memoirs, I Married the World *(1955):*

Envious Europeans didn't realize they indicted themselves in ridiculing the blunders of American social climbers they courted assiduously. Mrs Kate Moore, the wife of a Mid-Western tycoon, was a laughingstock for her malapropisms, yet the upper crust scrambled for invitations to her lavish salons. Once she entertained King Edward VII, who admired her sculpture. 'Oh, wait until you see the lovely bust of my hands I've commissioned,' Mrs Moore said grandly.

Although most of England's great fortunes still were intact, practically anyone who dispensed food and drink with a free hand was a social success in pre-World-War-I London. Ethel Levey, the divorced wife of George M. Cohan, who was appearing in *Hullo Ragtime*, a revue, still is remembered as the Woman Who Fed Mayfair. She established such high standards of hospitality that more than one American later went broke in London trying to pull an Ethel Levey. Even Elsie Janis's mother, a thrifty Ohio housewife, went overboard in buying her way into British society. When Lord Lonsdale, the well-known sportsman, dined at her home, Mrs Janis was so impressed that she told her butler, 'John, dear, fetch a seventy-five-cent Corona for the noble Lord.'

Another such American lady was Mrs Corrigan. Arriving in England, she took Mrs George Keppel's house in Grosvenor Street – she is said to have referred to it as 'my little ventre-à-terre' *– and asked the owner to include*

her guest list in the lease. Mrs Keppel, we are told, rose worthily to the occasion by granting the request and raising the rent. Mrs Corrigan made her way by a very subtle form of bribery, giving splendid prizes at her cotillons: dukes won coroneted sock suspenders, others got initialled braces with solid gold tabs. It was said that when she was asked if, on a Mediterranean cruise, she had seen the Dardanelles, the artless arriviste *replied 'I had a letter of introduction to them, but I didn't use it.'*

👑

Elsa Maxwell herself earns a mention for the truly snobbish caption to a photograph in her autobiography: beneath a grinning group is written

At the Café de Paris, with Noel Coward, two Rothschilds, a princess and Lady Mendl.

It is in this world that we find ourselves in Anita Loos's Gentlemen Prefer Blondes (*1925*). *Lorelei Lee and her friend Dorothy, campaigning in London, meet an English gentleman, Sir Francis Beekman, whom Lorelei calls 'Piggie', and from whom she eventually extracts a diamond tiara.*

Piggie really likes to talk quite a lot and he is always talking about a friend of his who was quite a famous King in London called King Edward. So Piggie said he would never never forget the jokes King Edward was always saying and he would never forget one time they were all on a yacht and they were all sitting at a table and King Edward got up and said 'I don't care what you gentlemen do – I'm going to smoke a cigar.' So then Piggie laughed very, very loud. So of course I laughed very, very loud and I told Piggie he was wonderful the way he could tell jokes. I mean you can always tell when to laugh because Piggie always laughs first.

AWKWARD RELATIONS

From such crudities it is time to turn back to a more genuine article, and that title cannot be refused to the fourth Earl of Chesterfield (1694–1773). His relentless letters of instruction to his natural son Philip Stanhope, whom he vainly tried to mould into a fine gentleman, form one of the minor comedies of the eighteenth century. A couple of extracts give the flavour:

Having mentioned laughing, I must particularly warn you against it: and I could heartily wish that you may often be seen to smile, but never heard to laugh. Frequent and loud laughter is the characteristic of folly and ill manners: it is the manner in which the mob express their silly joy at silly things . . . in my mind there is nothing so illiberal, and so ill-bred, as audible laughter.

I must insist upon your neither piping nor fiddling yourself. It puts a gentleman in a very frivolous, contemptible light . . . Few things would mortify me more, than to see you bearing a part in a concert, with a fiddle under your chin, or a pipe in your mouth.

Unfortunately young Philip was an awkward booby, who never acquired any polish at all. We read of a great dinner at Chesterfield House, after the young man's return to England, the table covered with brilliant silver and rich delicacies. Philip fell in love with 'an oval silver dish containing a quantity of excellent baked gooseberries, then a rarity, snowed over with a rich covering of whipped cream.' After one large helping he called back the servant who was removing it, held the dish, foaming with cream, under his chin, and 'lapped it up in hasty spoonfuls'. Lord Chesterfield had the mortification of seeing his son the object of the astonished gaze of the company. Concealing his chagrin, he said to Philip's valet, 'John, why

[30]

do you not fetch the strop and the razors? You see your master is going to shave himself'. If snobbishness has its martyrs, then at that moment Lord Chesterfield was one of them.

♔

Meredith begins The Egoist *with a noble example of the Cut as administered by a person of whom Chesterfield would have approved. Sir Willoughby Patterne is a snob of distinguished style.*

The country and the chief of this family were simultaneously informed of the existence of one Lieutenant Crossjay Patterne, of the corps of the famous hard fighters, through an act of heroism of the unpretending cool sort which kindles British blood, on the part of the modest young officer, in the storming of some eastern riverain stronghold, somewhere about the coast of China. The officer's youth was assumed on the strength of his rank, perhaps likewise from the tale of his modesty: 'he had only done his duty'. Our Willoughby was then at College, emulous of the generous enthusiasm of his years, and strangely impressed by the report, and the printing of his name in the newspapers. He thought over it for several months, when, coming to his title and heritage, he sent Lieutenant Crossjay Patterne a cheque for a sum of money amounting to the gallant fellow's pay per annum, at the same time showing his acquaintance with the first, or chemical, principles of generosity, in the remark to friends at home, that 'blood is thicker than water'. The man is a Marine, but he is a Patterne. How any Patterne should have drifted into the Marines, is of the order of questions which are senselessly asked of the great dispensary. In the complimentary letter accompanying his cheque, the lieutenant was invited to present himself at the ancestral Hall, when convenient to him, and he was assured that he had given his relative and friend a taste for a soldier's life. Young Sir Willoughby was fond of talking of his 'military namesake and distant cousin, young Patterne – the Marine'.

He was one afternoon parading between showers on the stately garden terrace of the Hall, in company with his affianced, the beautiful and dashing Constantia Durham, followed by knots of ladies and gentlemen vowed to fresh air before dinner, while it was to be had. Chancing with his usual happy fortune (we call these things dealt to us out of the great hidden dispensary, chance) to glance up the avenue of limes, as he was in the act of turning on his heel at the end of the terrace, and, it should be added, discoursing with passion's privilege of the passion of love to Miss Durham, Sir Willoughby, who was anything but obtuse, experienced a presentiment upon espying a thickset stumpy man crossing the gravel space from the avenue to the front steps of the Hall, decidedly *not* bearing the stamp of the gentleman 'on his hat, his coat, his feet, or anything that was his,' Willoughby subsequently observed to the ladies of his family in the Scriptural style of gentlemen who do bear the stamp. His brief sketch of the creature was repulsive. The visitor carried a bag, and his coat-collar was up, his hat was melancholy; he had the appearance of a bankrupt tradesman absconding; no gloves, no umbrella.

As to the incident we have to note, it was very slight. The card of Lieutenant Patterne was handed to Sir Willoughby, who laid it on the salver, saying to the footman, 'Not at home . . . '

Young Sir Willoughby spoke a word of the rejected visitor to Miss Durham, in response to her startled look: 'I shall drop him a cheque,' he said, for she seemed personally wounded, and had a face of crimson.

The young lady did not reply.

Snobbishness within the family is a special branch of the subject. The memoirs of Captain Gronow, M.P. and duellist, which deal with the age of the dandies of the Regency, contribute an elegant example.

In London in those days a worldly man or woman would, without scruple, cut their father or mother, did they not belong to the particular set which they considered good society. Mr S— was once riding in the Park with the Marquis of C—, then one of the kings of the fashionable world, and some other dandies of that day, when they met a respectable-looking elderly man, who nodded somewhat familiarly to S—. 'Who's your friend?' drawled Lord C—. 'That?' replied S—; 'oh, a very good sort of fellow, one of my Cheshire farmers.' It was his own father; a most amiable and excellent man, and who had better blood in his veins than any of the lordlings by whom his unworthy son was surrounded.

R. H. Gronow, *Reminiscences*, 1862

Anyone who has ever been an adolescent and had to introduce his parents and his friends will have some understanding of this ignoble feeling; and it may be that the discomfort which assails us in the monkey-house is a manifestation of this same unease at the presence of discreditable kinsmen.

It is just as possible to feel ashamed of one's friends in front of one's family, as to be mortified by one's family in the presence of one's friends. Here, in Auberon Waugh's novel The Foxglove Saga *(1960), two schoolboys are getting ready to go home together for the holidays; the problem is that one of them is the son of a knight.*

Stoat was wondering what on earth he should call Lady Foxglove. His father, although a bore, and a man in whose company he had never been comfortable, was one of the best dentists in Nottingham, although these snobbish fools didn't know it. Nevertheless, while his practice took him among the privileged and great of Nottingham, his social life did not, for some reason, include anybody with a title, or 'handle' as he liked to put it. 'Your Ladyship' sounded a bit pompous, and 'My Lady' a bit familiar.

'What time did her Ladyship say she'd be arriving, Foxy?' he asked to try it out.

'For Heaven's sake, don't call her that,' answered the other, alarmed.

'What should I call her then?'

'Oh, don't call her anything. And you'd better call me Martin, I suppose,' he added, a shade too carelessly. 'Though goodness knows what I'm going to call you. Kenneth would not go down at all, I'm afraid.'

'My father calls me Ken,' said Kenneth miserably. Martin was a kind boy at heart, and he did not pounce on this as he might have. Instead he stored it up for their next quarrel.

'I think I'd better say you're called Henry,' he said.

From the seventeenth century Congreve, in The Way of the World, *shows the particular chagrin caused to a man who has become fashionable in London, when his elder brother, an unfashionable country knight, suddenly appears in a London drawing-room.*

MRS MARWOOD. Don't you know this Gentleman, Sir?
SIR WILFULL WITWOUD. Hum! What, sure 'tis not – Yea by'r Lady, but 'tis – 'Sheart I know not whether 'tis or no – Yea, but 'tis, by the *Rekin*. Brother *Antony*! What *Tony*, i'faith! What dost thou not know me? By'r Lady nor I thee, thou art so Becravated, and so Beperriwig'd – 'Sheart, why dost not speak? Art thou o'erjoy'd?
WITWOUD. Odso Brother, is it you? Your Servant, Brother.

SIR WILFULL WITWOUD. Your Servant! Why yours, Sir.
Your Servant again – 'Sheart, and your Friend and
Servant to that – And a – (*puff*) and a Flap Dragon
for your Service, Sir: And a Hare's Foot, and a
Hare's Scut for your Service, Sir; an you be so cold
and so courtly!

WITWOUD. No Offence, I hope, Brother.

SIR WILFULL WITWOUD. 'Sheart, Sir, but there is, and
much Offence – A Pox, is this your Inns o'Court
Breeding, not to know your Friends and your Relations, your Elders, and your Betters?

WITWOUD. Why, Brother *Wilfull of Salop*, you may be
as short as a *Shrewsbury* Cake, if you please. But I
tell you 'tis not modish to know Relations in Town.
You think you're in the Country, where great
lubberly Brothers slabber and kiss one another when
they meet, like a Call of Serjeants – 'Tis not the
Fashion here; 'tis not indeed, dear Brother.

SIR WILFULL WITWOUD. The Fashion's a Fool; and
you're a Fop, dear Brother. 'Sheart, I suspected this;
By'r Lady I conjectur'd you were a Fop, since you
began to change the Stile of your Letters, and write
in a scrap of Paper gilt round the Edges, no bigger
than a *Subpoena*. I might expect this when you left
off, Honour'd Brother; and hoping you are in good
Health, and so forth – To begin with a Rat me,
Knight, I'm so sick of a last Night's Debauch – Od's
Heart, and then tell a familiar Tale of a Cock and a
Bull, and a Whore and a Bottle, and so conclude –
You cou'd write News before you were out of your
Time, when you liv'd with honest *Pumple Nose* the
Attorney of *Furnival's* Inn – you cou'd intreat to be
remember'd then to your Friends round the *Rekin*.

PETULANT. 'Slife, *Witwoud*, were you ever an Attorney's
Clerk? Of the Family of the *Furnivals*. Ha, ha, ha!

WITWOUD. Ay, ay, but that was but for a while. Not

long, not long; pshaw, I was not in my own Power then. An Orphan, and this Fellow was my Guardian; ay, ay, I was glad to consent to that Man to come to *London*. He had the Disposal of me then. If I had not agreed to that, I might have been bound Prentice to a Felt-maker in *Shrewsbury*; this Fellow would have bound me to a Maker of Felts.

SIR WILFULL WITWOUD. 'Sheart, and better than to be bound to a Maker of Fops; where, I suppose, you have served your Time; and now you may set up for your self.

The laugh is perhaps on the father in the story told of Alexandre Dumas père. *He was the son of a native of the French West Indies, very dark in complexion, and with woolly hair. His son, Alexandre Dumas* fils, *said that his father was so mean, and also so ostentatious, that*

I am always expecting him to get up behind his own carriage, in order to make people think he has a negro footman.

When Evelyn Waugh, after a dinner at which one of his fellow guests was his host's publisher, said 'Next time I suppose we shall dine with your butcher', he doubtless knew that his friends remembered that he was himself a publisher's son. More deeply snobbish was the response of the young Bernard Berenson, who had spent his first nine years in a Lithuanian ghetto, but who as a young Harvard man was pretending a mere supercilious ignorance about Jews –

We need to study so that we shall begin to understand the puzzling character of the Jews; begin to understand them, I say, for comprehend them we never shall. Their character and their interests are too vitally opposed to ours . . .

Visiting his rich but all too Jewish relatives in Berlin,

[36]

he was repelled by the unrhythmic movements of the faithful in the synagogue.

Undoubtedly they were selling old clothes to each other *he wrote to his patron, Isabella Stewart Gardner.*

But the furthest point of this sort of snobbishness was achieved by the Emperor Caligula. He, we are told, was so much ashamed of being the grandson of Augustus' daughter by the ancestor-less Agrippa, that he preferred to claim that Agrippa had no part in his procreation, but that Augustus had incestuously violated his own daughter. The preference for descent from a crime by a noble rather than a respectable union with a commoner marks, perhaps, the point where snobbishness blends into madness.

THE SNOB AT COURT

The divinity that doth hedge a king is, to mix my metaphor, a rich loam for the growth of exotic flowers of snobbishness. The next two passages, both the work of literary ladies who were also courtiers, exemplify this, and I think they have a lot in common. Sei Shonagon, a lady at the Japanese court in the 990s AD and one of the most distinguished writers in Japanese literature, becomes at moments, where the Imperial Family is concerned, quite silly. She writes of an occasion where the Emperor's brother paraded in the uniform of a new court position:

I imagined the feelings of the Dowager Empress as she watched her son pass by with his retinue. My heart leapt with joy, and tears came to my eyes – much to the amusement of the people who were watching me. Even common people are delighted if things go well for their children; when one imagines what the Empress Dowager must have felt, it is really awe-inspiring.

The Pillow-Book of Sei Shonagon, trans. Ivan Morris, 1967

Secondly, Madame d'Arblay, who as Fanny Burney had
written the best-loved novel of her generation, who had
been the friend of Dr Johnson, of Reynolds and of Burke,
describes her presentation to Louis XVIII; the royal lips
ennoble the English language and England itself.

His majesty took his seat, with an air of mingled sweet-
ness and dignity. I then, being immediately behind
him, lost sight of his countenance, but saw that of every
individual who approached to be presented. The Duc
de Duras stood at his left hand, and was *le grand*
maître des cérémonies. . . .

Early in this ceremony came forward Lady Crewe,
who being known to the king from sundry previous
meetings, was not named; and only, after curtseying,
reciprocated smiles with his majesty, and passed on.
But instead of then moving off, though the duke, who
did not know her, waved his hand to hasten her away,
she whispered, but loud enough for me to hear, 'There
is Madame d'Arblay; she must be presented.' She then
went gaily off, without heeding me.

The duke only bowed, but by a quick glance recognised me, and by another showed a pleased acquies-
cence in the demand.

Retreat, now, was out of the question; but I so feared
my position was wrong, that I was terribly disturbed,
and felt hot and cold, and cold and hot, alternately,
with excess of embarrassment. I was roused, however,
after hearing for so long a time nothing but French, by
the sudden sound of English. An address, in that
language, was read to his majesty, which was presented
by the noblemen and gentlemen of the county of
Buckingham, congratulatory upon his happy restora-
tion, and filled with cordial thanks for the graciousness
of his manners, and the benignity of his conduct,
during his long residence amongst them; warmly pro-

claiming their participation in his joy, and their admiration of his virtues. The reader was Colonel Nugent, a near relation of the present Duke of Buckingham.

But, if the unexpected sound of these felicitations, delivered in English, roused and struck me, how much greater arose my astonishment and delight when the French monarch, in an accent of the most condescending familiarity and pleasure, uttered his acknowledgements in English also – expressing his gratitude for all their attentions, his sense of their kind interest in his favour, and his eternal remembrance of the obligations he owed to the whole county of Buckinghamshire, for the asylum and consolations he had found in it during his trials and calamities!

I wonder not that Colonel Nugent was so touched by this reply, as to be led to bend the knee, as to his own sovereign, when the king held out his hand; for I myself, though a mere outside auditress, was so moved, and so transported with surprise by the dear English language from his mouth, that I forgot at once all my fears, and dubitations, and, indeed all *myself*, my poor little *self*, in my pride and exultation at such a moment for my noble country.

Fanny Burney, *Diary*, 1842–6

The bitter Chamfort reports:

Amid the disasters of the end of the reign of Louis XIV, after the defeats at Turin, Oudenarde, Malplaquet, Ramillies, and Hochstet, the most respected people about the court used to say, 'At least the king is in good health; that is the main thing'.

Maximes, caractères et anecdotes

Cards of invitation from royalty are things which many people like to show off. The poet Samuel Rogers was that rarest of beings, a wealthy poet, living in luxury on his family banking business. Sydney Smith, seeing over his chimney-piece a fine display of them, said,

'Does it not look as if the bank had been accommodating the Duchess of Kent?'

But sometimes even royal persons could be disconcerted by the vagaries of snobbishness in those who surrounded them. 'Chips' Channon records

We had a scratch dinner party (31 November [*sic*] 1937) which included Emerald Cunard and Fritzi (the Crown Prince) of Prussia. The latter looked surprised when Emerald said, 'Monseigneur, which do you think the more unfashionable, the Connaughts or the Gloucesters?'

I conclude this opening section with two general passages, one English, one American. It is noteworthy that the American is cast in terms of money, the English in terms which are different and which indeed conflict with the pecuniary standard. That has always been the European way. In the fifth century BC the poet Simonides was asked for the definition of nobility; when he gave the answer 'Inherited wealth', he was thought to have said something exceedingly cynical, for which neither contemporaries nor posterity forgave him.

From BESIDE THE SEASIDE, by John Betjeman

. . . Whether we like to sit with Penguin books
In sheltered alcoves farther up the cliff,
Or to eat winkles on the Esplanade,
Or to play golf along the crowded course,
Or on a twopenny borough council chair
To doze away the strains of *Humoresque*,
Adapted for the cornet and the drums
By the conductor of the Silver Band,
Whether we own a tandem or a Rolls,
Whether we Rudge it or we trudge it, still
A single topic occupies our minds.
'Tis hinted at or boldly blazoned in
Our accents, clothes and ways of eating fish,
And being introduced and taking leave,
'Farewell,' 'So long,' 'Bunghosky,'
    'Cheeriby' –
That topic all-absorbing, as it was,
Is now and ever shall be, to us – CLASS.

Mr and Mrs Stephen Grosvenor-Smith
(He manages a Bank in Nottingham)
Have come to Sandy Cove for thirty years,
And now they think the place is going down.

'Not what is was, I'm very much afraid.
Look at that little mite with *Attaboy*
Printed across her paper sailor hat.
Disgusting, isn't it? Who *can* they be,
Her parents, to allow such forwardness?'

The Browns, who thus are commented
    upon,
Have certainly done very well indeed.
The elder children bringing money in,
Father still working; with allowances
For this and that and little income-tax,
They probably earn seven times as much

As poor old Grosvenor-Smith. But who will
   grudge
Them this, their wild, spontaneous holiday?
The morning paddle, then the mystery tour
By motor-coach inland this afternoon.
For that old mother what a happy time!
At last past bearing children, she can sit
Reposeful on a crowded bit of beach.
A week of idleness, the salty winds
Play in her greying hair; the summer sun
Puts back her freckles so that Alfred Brown
Remembers courting days in Gospel Oak
And takes her to the Flannel Dance to-night.
But all the same they think the place
   'Stuck up',
And Blackpool, next year – if there *is*
   a next. . . .

The American passage, from Scott Fitzgerald's story
The Rich Boy, *puts a gloss on what Fitzgerald meant in
his notorious exchange with Hemingway: 'The rich are
different from us.' – 'Yes, they have more money.' He says,
at the opening of the story,*

Let me tell you about the very rich. They are different
from you and me. They possess and enjoy early, and
it does something to them, makes them soft where we
are hard, and cynical where we are trustful, in a way
that, unless you were born rich, it is very difficult to
understand. They think, deep in their hearts, that they
are better than we are because we had to discover the
compensation and refuges of life for ourselves. Even
when they enter deep into our world or sink below us,
they still think that they are better than we are. They
are different.

Academic Snobs

An Oxford book of snobs would be missing an obvious target and failing in an evident duty if it did not look at academic snobbery. There was a time when this was entirely undisguised, as we see from the record which the Public Orator of the University of Oxford made of the events which led to the expulsion from St Edmund Hall, and from the University, of six men accused of low origins, Methodism, and ignorance – in that order, it seems – in 1768.

James Matthews – accused that he was brought up to the trade of a weaver – that he had kept a taphouse – confessed. Thomas Jones – accused that he had been brought up to the trade of a barber, which he had followed very lately – confessed.

And so on. He concludes:

The legal or statutable cause of their expulsion was their having attended illegal conventicles, prohibited by the Statutes of the University . . . A farther aggravation of their crime was that they were most of them illiterate mechanics, who had intruded themselves into the University, for which they were neither designed nor qualified.

Oxford in the eighteenth century was not to be defiled by the presence of such people.

♕

In the early years of this century, when it was no longer possible to take quite so firm a line, fondness for birth and rank still lingered in the minds of some Oxford dons. The famous Dr Blakiston, President of Trinity College, Oxford, from 1907 to 1938, yields an anecdote full of period flavour.

His unquestioning belief in the nobility as patterns of refined taste and moral sensibility sometimes verged on the ridiculous. One day during my deanship he complained to me about a noisy party held somewhere near the Lodgings on the previous night. I explained that the Eight had been celebrating the end of training in the rooms of the elder Bathurst, who was one of their number and the son of a noble house long associated with Trinity. Blakiston seemed a little put out at this report. 'What were they singing?' he asked. 'The usual things', I said, 'including marching-songs common to their generation, some of them rather bawdy.' 'That', he replied, 'must have been most distasteful to Bathurst' – words which soon became a Common Room cliché . . .

T. F. Higham, *Dr. Blakiston Recalled,* 1967

It is a sad fact that the love felt by such dons for the aristocracy was by no means always reciprocated with equal fervour. Lord Hervey, for instance, in his Memoirs *(1848), is decidedly unsentimental, as we see in the following passage about Lord Isla, brother of the Duke of Argyll.*

Lord Isla was the man on whom Sir Robert Walpole depended entirely for the management of all Scottish affairs; a man of parts, quickness, knowledge, temper, dexterity, and judgment – a man of little truth, little honour, little principle, and no attachment but to his interest. A pedantic, dirty, shrewd, unbred fellow of a college with a mean aspect, bred to the sophistry of the civil law, and made a peer, would have been just such a man.

Oscar Browning (1837–1923), a Fellow of King's, Cambridge, and a man celebrated in his day, was well known for his cultivation of the great. We find a charming story of his behaviour on a visit, towards the end of his life, to Rome.

He paid a visit of respect to the widowed Queen Margherita. She was out, but a fancy drain-pipe, which served as a receptacle for cards, was indicated to us, and into it he dropped his. I was about to do the same when he checked me, saying 'My dear boy, she's never heard of you.' Riding back in our cardinal's carriage I fell asleep, to be aroused by the movements of O.B., who suddenly leaped from the seat and bowed many times. The Queen turned towards him, and O.B. said, 'Did you notice what attention she paid to me?' I thought it not surprising, but said nothing . . .

H. E. Wortham, *Victorian Eton and Cambridge*

This poor man was also the recipient of one of the most crushing snubs in history. When Tennyson came on a state visit to Cambridge, Oscar Browning bustled up, hand held out, with the words 'I'm Browning.' 'No you're not!' came the unanswerable reply.

That extraordinary man Professor Max Mueller, P.C., who established himself at Oxford as supreme pundit on the languages and religions of the East, was said to have murmured, in an ecstasy of royalism,

The *nicest* Emperor I know is Germany . . .

But his snobbishness came up against a harder and greater one, when Theodor Mommsen, the master of Roman historians, asked an English friend,

Have you no humbugs in your country, that you import them from mine?

[45]

J. P. Mahaffy, a classical scholar who for many years was a great figure at Trinity College, Dublin, had the same weakness for crowned heads. On a trip to Greece he was made a present of a dog by a lady related to the King of that country, to his great pleasure. When the dog died, Oliver St John Gogarty wrote a threnody in the style of Swinburne, On the Death of Diogenes, the Doctor's Dog.

> As I wambled awound
>> On the gwound that was Gweece
> I was given that hound
>> By the King's little niece,
> And had rather be fined e'er I found him,
>> To gaze on his saddest surcease.

(Chorus of Scholars)
> He was given that hound
>> By the seed of a King,
> For the wisdom profound
>> of his wide wandering.
> But was it the owner, or donor,
>> Or dog that was led on a string?

The hero of Trollope's novel The Claverings (*1867*), *a gentleman who has been a Fellow of a Cambridge College, falls in love with the daughter of an engineer, and finds himself working in the family firm. The company grates upon his self-esteem, and the reader is not surprised when he takes to neglecting his bourgeois betrothed for an aristocratic siren.*

Nothing could be nicer than his room, or more pleasant than the table and seat which he was to occupy near a window; but there was something in the tone of the other men towards him which did not quite satisfy him. They probably did not know that he was a fellow of a college, and treated him almost as they might have done had he come to them direct from King's College, in the Strand, or from the London University. Down at Stratton, a certain amount of honour had been paid to him. They had known there who he was, and had felt some deference for him. They had not slapped him on the back, or poked him in the ribs, or even called him old fellow, before some length of acquaintance justified such appellation. But up at Mr Beilby's, 'in the Adelphi, one young man, who was certainly his junior in age, and who did not seem as yet to have attained any high position in the science of engineering, manifestly thought that he was acting in a friendly and becoming way by declaring the stranger to be a lad of wax on the second day of his appearance. . . .

There was a man at Mr Beilby's, who was entitled to greet him with endearing terms, and to be so greeted himself, although Harry had never seen him till he attended for the first time at the Adelphi. This was Theodore Burton, his future brother-in-law, who was now the leading man in the London house:—the leading man as regarded business, though he was not as yet a partner. It was understood that this Mr Burton was to come in when his father went out; and in the meantime he received a salary of a thousand a year as managing clerk. A very hard-working, steady, intelligent man was Mr Theodore Burton, with a bald head, a high forehead, and that look of constant work about him which such men obtain. Harry Clavering could not bring himself to take a liking to him, because he wore cotton gloves and had an odious habit of dusting his shoes with his pocket-handkerchief. Twice Harry saw him do this on the first day of their acquaintance, and he regretted it exceedingly. The cotton gloves too were offensive, as were also the thick shoes which had been dusted; but the dusting was the great sin.

Academic snobbishness could also take other and more academic forms. Of Dr Jenkyns, Master of Balliol, we read that

his regard for his own dignity was very great. Once he slipped and fell as he was returning from a walk, and two undergraduates rushed to help him up. As they were laying their hands on him, he saw an M.A. approaching and cried out, 'Stop, I see a Master of Arts coming down the street.' Helped on to his legs by the M.A., he dismissed the undergraduates with thanks ...

N. C. Chaudhuri, *Scholar Extraordinary*, 1974

It can be turned to delighted contemplation, not of one's superiority to other members of one's own institution, but of the superiority of one's own institution as a whole to any other. The secret society of the Apostles in Cambridge was firmly convinced of this. Michael Holroyd, in his biography of Lytton Strachey writes, of the Apostles:

Venables would often extemporise with genuine amazement on their good fortune at being exalted so far above the general rank and file of humanity, and wonder why in heaven they had been gifted to such excess over 'those cursed idiotic oxford (they spelt the hated word with a tiny 'o') brutes'. And Strachey, too, felt something of the same fiercely partisan convictions, lamenting over the rival University like Christ over Jerusalem.

Michael Holroyd, *Lytton Strachey: a Critical Biography*, I, 1967

And who, asks the reader, was the so gifted Venables? Alas, it appears from the same source that he 'failed to achieve any form of distinction whatever'.

Between academic subjects, too, hierarchies could be constructed. Here Evelyn Waugh speaks of his schooldays at Lancing.

[48]

In school we demonstrated our contempt for 'stinks' and our resentment that we, on the classical side, should be required to study them once or twice a week. Scientists were regarded as a socially inferior race and we treated our masters in these subjects superciliously. We also had much innocent fun in causing explosions in the laboratories. These men tried to make a fetish of the weights in the glass-enclosed scales. We were forbidden to touch them with our fingers lest we corrupted their accuracy. We used to heat them on bunsen-burners and drop them sizzling into beakers of cold water.

Evelyn Waugh, *A Little Learning*, 1964

The Snob & the Arts

Not only academics but also other men of letters come into contact with high society. Often the aristocracy of talent was overwhelmed by the aristocracy of birth. Stendhal comments grimly:

The genius of an upstart does not protect him against the influence of rank. We see Rousseau falling in love with all the *ladies* he met, and crying with rapture because the Duc de Luxembourg, one of the most stupid courtiers of his time, deigned to walk on the right of the street rather than the left, in order to accompany M. Coindet, a friend of Rousseau.

Stendhal on Love, trans H.B.V., 1927

It seems that this veneration of Rousseau for the great was not universally returned. Chamfort tells us:

At the time of the great quarrel between Diderot and Rousseau, M. de Castries said with impatience, 'It's unbelievable! The world talks of nothing but those people, who have no property, who have not even a house, but lodge in a garret. One just cannot get used to it.'

Maximes, caractères et anecdotes

Lady Mary Wortley Montagu, one of the most intelligent women of her time and the author of works in prose and verse, expressed in pungent form the contempt of her aristocratic order for the writer, even the writer of genius.

Her insistence that she had never published anything under her name was an expression of her aristocratic code that a person of quality should never turn author. This was allied to another class standard, that writing for money made it a 'trade'. She enunciated the lofty belief that one of 'the most distinguishing prerogatives of mankind, writing, when duly executed' did honour to human nature, and that it was contemptible if done for the purpose of making money. As she grew older, her other aristocratic principles ossified. She especially condemned the 'levelling principle' which exalted the lower classes. 'I wish to God I had always thought in the same manner,' she exclaimed; 'yet the silly prejudices of my education had taught me to believe I was to treat nobody as an inferior, and that poverty was a degree of merit: this imaginary humility has made me admit many familiar acquaintances, of which I have heartily repented every one, and the greatest examples I have known of honour and integrity have been among those of the highest birth and fortunes.'

R. Halsband, *The Life of Lady Mary Wortley Montagu*, 1956

Her views were so reactionary, she realized, that if they were known she would be called an arrogant enemy of the poor. She particularly condemned Swift and Pope who 'by their birth and hereditary fortune' deserved to be only a couple of footmen.

In this century there has been a tendency to feel that intellectuals, not peers, are the true aristocracy. A strikingly old-fashioned exception, which perhaps even Lady Mary would have found a little shrill, is provided by G. Coquiot, who tells us that into the Hôtel Biron, that great house, in the early years of the twentieth century there

rushed an uproarious horde, and soon every chink and corner was crawling with their lice . . . painters and sculptors mostly, so wretchedly mediocre that sometimes, even now, long after they have been got rid of, the Hôtel Biron stinks of their putrid filth . . .

Rodin à l'hôtel de Biron et à Meudon, 1917

This frightful crew included Cocteau, Isadora Duncan, Matisse, and Rilke.

♔

Lady Ottoline Morrell, sister of the Duke of Portland, was a great patron of writers and artists, and her house at Garsington was always full of them; but if her brother came to see her, Bohemia was kept firmly upstairs, her ladyship tantalizing them with the whispered message, 'Portland's downstairs'. It is pleasant to record that they took this sort of thing in good part, D. H. Lawrence writing to her, 'Don't abrogate one jot or tittle of your high birth . . .'

♔

We have seen Lawrence wish that he had been born an aristocrat. David Garnett, in The Golden Echo (*1953*), *gives us a description of him, in snobbish terms, which underlines the hopelessness of that wish.*

His hair was of a colour, and grew in a particular way, which I have never seen except in English working men. It was bright mud-colour, with a streak of red in it,

[52]

a thick mat, parted on one side. Somehow it was in-
credibly plebeian, mongrel and underbred . . . He was
the type of the plumber's mate who goes back to fetch
the tools. He was the weedy runt you find in every gang
of workmen.

*It is all the more touching that Lawrence gives to Lady
Chatterley's lover, the Lawrentian gamekeeper, something
even better:*

He had a natural distinction, but he had not the cut-
to-pattern look of her class . . . He had a native breeding
which was really much nicer than the cut-to-pattern
class thing.

Harold Nicolson in his little book Some People (1927)
*has created an admirable figure of the aristocrat torn
between his rank and his art, in the Marquis de Chaumont;
in the First World War period of proletarian verse*

his muse walked the pavements with the others, but
she wore goloshes and was terribly afraid of being
recognised.

*Finally he is confronted with a great choice: immortality
from the pen of Proust, balanced by a fear that it may do
him harm socially, when he is hoping to be elected to the
Jockey Club.*

A few weeks later we heard that Proust was again
seriously ill. He had been working at *Pastiches et
Mélanges*, and the effort exhausted him. De Chaumont
came to see me in obvious tribulation, carrying a letter
in his hand. I read the letter. It was from Proust, saying
that he had written a short sketch in the manner of
Saint-Simon, and would Jacques mind if he figured in
it by name? The latter was embarrassed how to answer.
He did not wish to offend Proust, yet on the other hand,

well, really . . . I said that I, for my part, would have
been in the seventh heaven had Proust showed any
inclination to insert me in *Pastiches et Mélanges*.
De Chaumont said 'it moight be jolly well all roight for
a foreigner, but moy mother would not loike it'. I told
him that I had met his mother, and was convinced that
she would not mind in the least. He was only slightly
disconcerted. 'Then there is moy aunt, de Maubize.
She 'ates Jews.' I began to get a little angry at this, and
told him that I doubted whether Proust would live for
long, that he was the greatest living writer, that Jacques
was sacrificing a free gift of immortality, and that what
on earth could it matter about his aunt? He sat there
turning the letter over and over in his gloved hands.
Suddenly he tore it up with a gesture of decision: he
flung it into one of the large brass bowls that enlivened
the foyer of the Majestic.

'Non!' he said, 'non pas! Ça me ratera mon Jockey.'

The book appeared some months later and it contained no mention of Jacques de Chaumont. And the
following year I met a member of the Jockey Club
and asked him whether de Chaumont had been elected.
He said that he had not been elected.

*The society of the great can lead writers to believe that
they are great themselves. Gogarty said of Yeats in his
later years, as the poet identified himself increasingly with
the Ascendancy,*

Yeats is becoming so aristocratic, he's evicting imaginary tenants.

*Such presumption of equality could on occasion be harshly
dispelled. The young Voltaire came into a fashionable
drawing room with the words 'Are we all princes or all
poets?' – a question soon to be brutally answered when
the Chevalier de Rohan arranged for him to be called out*

*of just such a room and beaten up. Voltaire had taken his
acceptance so seriously as to answer the Chevalier back.
With the true attitude of his class towards the artist, he
instructed his bravoes:*

Spare his head; that may still do us some service.

*The attitude of Voltaire's grand friends to this event was
to close ranks; as one of them coolly observed, 'We should
be in a sad position if poets had no backs.'*

*The service of the cruel god Chic could expose a devotee to
fire from several sides at once. Between the Wars Lady
Colefax was one of the most prominent figures in Society,
an indefatigable hostess and also an aspiring patroness of
the arts. From the aristocratic side Lord Berners said of
her that when he stayed in the next room to hers in Rome,
it was impossible to sleep:*

She never stopped climbing all night.

*From another side she came up against a snobbishness no
less glacial and tremendous from the artists. Virginia
Woolf is exquisitely feline:*

I can't get a single friend of mine to meet her; no
painter, at any rate; because they know, a thousand
miles off, that she is tainted, tarred, corrupt, or whatever they call it. But I like a little high meat – in proof
of which, I have to go and see [Princess] Elizabeth
Bibesco . . .

The Letters of Virginia Woolf, ed. Nigel Nicolson

*When poor Lady Colefax showed signs of human sensi-
tivity, Virginia Woolf felt an Olympian amusement,
writing to Jacques Raverat:*

Then, socially, what about Lady Colefax? Being the
most successful, hardest-mouthed hostess in London,
she retains spots about the size of a sixpenny piece of

astonishing sensibility on her person. Having left her umbrella here, I, in malice or sport, proceeded to describe it, glowing and gleaming among my old gamps. Whereupon this hard bitten old hostess of 50 flushed quite red, and said 'Mrs Woolf, I know what you think of my umbrella – a cheap, stubby, vulgar umbrella, you think my umbrella: and you think I have a bag like it – a cheap flashy bag covered with bad embroidery.' And it was too true. Only, if she saw it, must there not be depths in Lady Colefax? Think this out, and let me know.

ibid.

Congreve, author of The Way of the World, *affected to be above mere authorship. When the young Voltaire came to see him, Congreve asked him to think of him not as a writer but simply as a gentleman.*

'If I had thought that,' *was the reply*, 'I should not have come to see you.'

If an author was of ignoble origins, reviewers might take pleasure in dwelling on them. The anonymous review of Keats in Blackwood's Edinburgh Magazine – *signed 'Z' – is a classic example.*

The just celebrity of Robert Burns and Miss Baillie has had the melancholy effect of turning the heads of we know not how many farm-servants and unmarried ladies; our very footmen compose tragedies . . . Mr. John Keats' friends, we understand, destined him to a career of medicine, and he was bound apprentice some years ago to a worthy apothecary in town . . . Precocious adulation confirmed the wavering apprentice in his desire to quit the gallipots . . . It is amusing to see what a hand the two Cockneys [Keats and Leigh Hunt] make of Greek mythology; the one confesses that he never read the Greek Tragedians, and the other knows

Homer only from Chapman; and both of them write about Apollo, Pan, Nymphs, Muses, and Mysteries, as might be expected from persons of their education . . . It is a better and a wiser thing to be a starved apothecary than a starved poet; so back to the shop, Mr. John, back to 'plasters, pills, and ointment boxes', etc. . . .

Since Byron was a lord and had been to Harrow, this charge could not be used against him. But it could be turned on his readers. The British Critic, *reviewing the later Cantos of* Don Juan, *observed that its circulation was now chiefly confined to*

that 'operative class', whose wives and daughters are their own housemaids.

♔

The exclusiveness of the intellectual and the artist should certainly not evade our scrutiny. It was raised to a dogma in the Nineties, so that for instance we find Oscar Wilde, in The Soul of Man under Socialism (*1891*), *writing*

The work of art is to dominate the spectator: the spectator is not to dominate the work of art. The spectator is to be receptive. He is to be the violin on which the master is to play. And the more completely he can suppress his own silly views, his own foolish prejudices, his own absurd ideas of what Art should or should not be, the more likely he is to understand and appreciate the work of art in question. This is, of course, quite obvious in the case of the vulgar theatre-going public of English men and women. But it is equally true of what are called educated people.

I have quoted before from Hints on Etiquette *of 1834. It is instructive to compare, with this passage of Wilde about the supremacy of artists, what that little book, two generations earlier, had to say about the peerage:*

We hear much of the courtesy, urbanity, and condescension of the aristocracy, and those who, in all humility, bow down, will experience it; but woe to the unfortunate wight, *who respects himself*, who dares to assert his own opinions in contradiction to theirs!

The distance between 'his own opinions' and 'his own foolish prejudices, his own absurd ideas' seems to suggest the greater hauteur and more complete contempt felt by the artist than the aristocrat.

♔

The painter Whistler used words which a duchess might have envied when he said

The one unspoken sympathy that pervades humanity is – Vulgarity!

And association with Wagner produced the same sort of feeling in the amiable Hans von Bülow. When there was criticism of his having taken out thirty seats from the Cuvilliés Theatre to enlarge the orchestra pit for Tristan, 'What does it matter', *cried the exasperated musician*, 'if we have thirty *Schweinhunde* more or less in the place?'

I quote from the Literary Essays *of Ezra Pound a passage which well conveys the flavour of intellectual élitism – interesting also as getting in, with elegant economy, a passing blow at his native country.*

Mr Hueffer is the best critic in England, one might say the only critic of any importance. What he says today the press, the reviewers who hate him and who disparage his books, will say in about nine years' time, or possibly sooner. Shelley, Yeats, Swinburne, with their 'unacknowledged legislators', with 'Nothing affects these people except our conversation', with 'The rest live under us'; Rémy de Gourmont, when he says that most men think only husks and shells of the thoughts that have already been lived over by others, have shown their very just appreciation of the system of echoes, of the general vacuity of public opinion. America is like England, America is very much what England would be with the two hundred most interesting people removed. One's life is the score of this two hundred with whom one happens to have made friends. I do not see that we need to say that the rest live under them, but it is certain that what these people say comes to pass.

The cinema has bred some noble snobs. 'Myles na Gopaleen' lets us hear one as he puts down a friend who likes ordinary Hollywood films:

Ah that's all right for you, I know the sort you are, but give me a private job that's shot on faded sepia sixteen millimetre stock with non-professional actors, epileptic cameramen, no story and dialogue in French *anny day of the week.*

The Best of Myles, ed. K. O'Nolan

It has been a recurrent idea that France is peculiarly the source of such cultural superiority. Aldous Huxley in Crome Yellow *(1921) gives us a charming vignette of this attitude.*

There was a discreet tap at the door. She looked up. 'Come in, come in.' A face, round and childish within its sleek bell of golden hair, peered round the opening door. More childish-looking still, a suit of mauve pyjamas made its entrance.

It was Mary. 'I thought I'd just look in for a moment to say good-night,' she said, and sat down on the edge of the bed.

Anne closed her book. 'That was very sweet of you.'

'What are you reading?' She looked at the book. 'Rather second-rate, isn't it?' The tone in which Mary pronounced the word 'second-rate' implied an almost infinite denigration. She was accustomed in London to associate only with first-rate people who liked first-rate things, and she knew that there were very few first-rate things in the world, and that those were mostly French.

'Well, I'm afraid I like it,' said Anne. There was nothing more to be said. The silence that followed was a rather uncomfortable one . . .

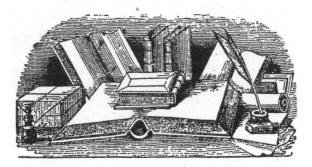

Changing Fashions

When romantic ideas come uppermost, the romantic can look down on the correct; W. M. Praed's charming poem, from which I select some verses, embodies one aspect of this scorn of the prosaic.

A LETTER OF ADVICE

*From Miss Medora Trevilian, at Padua, to
Miss Araminta Vavasour, in London*

> '*Enfin, monsieur, un homme aimable;
> Voilà pourquoi je ne saurais l'aimer.*' – Scribe

You tell me you're promised a lover,
  My own Araminta, next week;
Why cannot my fancy discover
  The hue of his coat and his cheek?
Alas! if he look like another,
  A vicar, a banker, a beau,
Be deaf to your father and mother,
  My own Araminta, say 'No!'

You know, when Lord Rigmarole's carriage
  Drove off with your cousin Justine,
You wept, dearest girl, at the marriage,
  And whispered 'How base she has been!'
You said you were sure it would kill you,
  If ever your husband looked so;
And you will not apostatise, – will you?
  My own Araminta, say 'No!'

SNOBS

If he wears a top-boot in his wooing,
  If he comes to you riding a cob,
If he talks of his baking or brewing,
  If he puts up his feet on the hob,
If he ever drinks port after dinner,
  If his brow or his breeding is low,
If he calls himself 'Thompson' or 'Skinner',
  My own Araminta, say 'No!'

If he studies the news in the papers
  While you are preparing the tea,
If he talks of the damps or the vapours
  While moonlight lies soft on the lea,
If his lips are not redder than roses,
  If his hands are not whiter than snow,
If he has not the model of noses, –
  My own Araminta, say 'No!'

If he speaks of a tax or a duty,
  If he does not look grand on his knees,
If he's blind to a landscape of beauty,
  Hills, valleys, rocks, waters, and trees,
If he dotes not on desolate towers,
  If he likes not to hear the blast blow,
If he knows not the language of flowers, –
  My own Araminta, say 'No!'

Don't listen to tales of his bounty,
  Don't hear what they say of his birth,
Don't look at his seat in the county,
  Don't calculate what he is worth;
But give him a theme to write verse on,
  And see if he turns out his toe;
If he's only an excellent person, –
  My own Araminta, say 'No!'

Poems, 1864

[62]

In another sort of society, it is the correct which deplores anything that savours of sensibility. Amy Dorrit, in Dickens's novel, is rebuked for excess of feeling and deficiency of correctness.

'Amy,' said Mr Dorrit, 'you have just now been the subject of some conversation between myself and Mrs General. We agree that you scarcely seem at home here. Ha – how is this?'

A pause.

'I think, father, I require a little time.'

'Papa is a preferable mode of address,' observed Mrs General. 'Father is rather vulgar, my dear. The word Papa, besides, gives a pretty form to the lips. Papa, potatoes, poultry, prunes, and prism are all very good words for the lips: especially prunes and prism. You will find it serviceable, in the formation of a demeanour, if you sometimes say to yourself in company – on entering a room, for instance – Papa, potatoes, poultry, prunes and prism, prunes and prism.'

'Pray, my child,' said Mr Dorrit, 'attend to the – hum – precepts of Mrs General.'

Poor Little Dorrit, with a rather forlorn glance at that eminent varnisher, promised to try . . .

Mrs General shut her eyes on being referred to; then, slowly opening them and rising, added these words:

'If Miss Amy Dorrit will direct her own attention to, and will accept of my poor assistance in, the formation of a surface, Mr Dorrit will have no further cause of anxiety. May I take this opportunity of remarking, as an instance in point, that it is scarcely delicate to look at vagrants with the attention which I have seen bestowed on them by a very dear young friend of mine? They should not be looked at. Nothing disagreeable should ever be looked at. Apart from such a habit

[63]

standing in the way of that graceful equanimity of surface which is so expressive of good-breeding, it hardly seems compatible with refinement of mind. A truly refined mind will seem to be ignorant of the existence of anything that is not perfectly proper, placid, and pleasant.' Having delivered this exalted sentiment, Mrs General made a sweeping obeisance, and retired with an expression of mouth indicative of Prunes and Prism.

Charles Dickens, *Little Dorrit*, 1857

Mrs General exemplifies one way of treating the problem of the poor; they are 'disagreeable', and a person of refinement will not look at them. This mid-Victorian attitude, too, has its late-Victorian counterpart in aestheticism, and again Wilde can give us an example – of regarding the poor not as an object of an aversion partly aesthetic and partly moral, but as a wholly aesthetic feature of the world, enjoyed rather than rejected.

'It is a sad fact,' *he writes in* London Models, 'but there is no doubt that the poor are completely unconscious of their own picturesqueness'.

From one point of view, the opposite attitude to that of Mrs General; but from another, a very similar one – and perhaps no less snobbish.

But aesthetic superiority is capable of another turn. Sei Shonagon presents another facet of the jewel when she lists among 'Unsuitable Things', 'Snow on the houses of common people. This is especially regrettable when the moonlight shines down on it.' The point here is that so picturesque an appearance was too good for them. She says in another place,

It is delightful when a man on horseback recites poetry at dawn. I remember that once I heard a splendid line of verse accompanied by the flapping of a horse's harness. Who could the rider be? When I put aside what I was doing and looked out, I was dismayed to see that he was a vulgar commoner.

The Pillow-Book of Sei Shonagon,
trans. Ivan Morris, 1967

We get a shock of a rather similar kind, perhaps, when we read such a triumph of aesthetic and social over moral considerations as the entry in the diary of 'Chips' Channon, as late as November 1936, about Hitler's Ambassador in London:

Later, Honor and I spoke to the Ribbentrops. My feeling is that they will not be a social success in London, though at first I prophesied great things for them; but, for all their ambition, they have not the well-bred ease which Londoners demand, and Frau von Ribbentrop really dresses too dowdily . . .

The habit of superiority can express itself in aesthetic terms, or it can be more bluntly practical. We find striking examples of the latter at many points in history: the assurance that those beneath us are not really human, need not be seriously considered. The following passage comes from a book on The Highlands and Western Isles of Scotland, *published in 1824 by Dr J. MacCulloch, F.R.S., on the effects of the evictions and forced emigration imposed on the Highlanders by their chiefs in the last two generations. Contemplating 'the former hamlets of the idle and useless population' of Sutherland, and their reluctance to be turned out, the Doctor observes:*

The attachment of the wretched creatures in question was a habit; the habit of indolence and inexperience, the attachment of an animal little differing in feeling from his own horned animals. Had it been even more, they were children, unable to judge for themselves, and knowing nothing beyond the narrow circle of their birth. As children, it was the duty of their superiors to judge for them, and to compel them for their own advantage.

Class

About 1,750 years earlier, Petronius had described his Trimalchio giving a Gargantuan dinner, grotesque in its extravagance, to a motley collection of people, many of them very hard up – 'Yesterday the company was much better, and I didn't give them nearly such good wine', remarks their host. They discuss the shocking price of bread and the way the producers combine to keep up the price of food. One of the guests starts a story: 'Once there were a rich man and a poor man, on bad terms with each other – ' 'What is a poor man?' Trimalchio interrupts. 'Very good!' laughs the impoverished guest . . .

The treatment of servants was a particular case. Could they really be human? Chamfort tells us the following as a true story about a daughter of the King of France:

As a child, playing with one of her maids, she looked at her hand, counting her fingers, and said, 'Why! Do you have five fingers too, just like me?' And she counted them again, to make sure.

Maximes, caractères et anecdotes

A neighbour of mine in Oxford, when her daily help once arranged to be picked up by a taxi, made her stand and wait for it on the pavement outside the house next door. A taxi could not come to her house for a servant.

Edmond de Goncourt, during the civil war in Paris in 1871, kept a journal of his experiences. On 23 May he watched two soldiers in the street outside risk death and die with great gallantry; he writes

I suppose that it has been given to few persons to witness two such heroic and such simple instances of contempt for death.

That night firing went on, and Goncourt observes

During a part of the night I am haunted by the terrible cries of a wounded soldier, who has dragged himself to our door, and whom the hall-porter has not allowed in, from a cowardly fear of compromising himself.

This anthology will hardly yield another piece of snobbishness as sublime as this; Goncourt, the passionate spectator of heroism, lying in bed and despising the porter – after all, it was his job to answer the door! – for failing to admit a wounded man. It could not cross his mind that he might do it himself.

Firbank set his last novel, The New Rhythm, *in New York. This light-hearted vignette is of a millionairess tipping a servant.*

Finding no ready coin in her pochette, (as, indeed, is not infrequent at all of an evening with ladies), she rewarded the page who procured the car with a condescending slap on the cheek with her cheque-book, and directed the chauffeur to the docks . . .

For hauteur we can hardly outstrip the Lady Sei Shonagon:

If a servant-girl says about someone 'What a delightful gentleman he is!' one immediately looks down on him, whereas if she insulted the person in question it would have the opposite effect. Praise from a servant can also damage a woman's reputation. Besides, people of that class always manage to express themselves badly when they are trying to say something nice.

The Pillow-Book of Sei Shonagon,
trans. Ivan Morris, 1967

The scorn of the gentleman for the servant and the artisan becomes, with Plato, part of an elaborate and universal philosophic scheme. When noble natures are seduced away from philosophy, which should be their concern, 'especially if a man comes from a powerful city and is wealthy and well-born within it, and also handsome and tall' (a very Greek addition), turning instead to the ephemeral pursuit of political power, then poor philosophy is left to pretenders. 'Little men', their souls stunted by ignoble occupations as their bodies are marred by their arts and crafts, take her up; and

the picture they present is just that of a little bald-headed tinker who has got rich and gained his freedom, and who, freshly bathed and wearing new clothes, is about to marry his master's daughter, who has fallen into poverty and neglect.

Plato (*c*. 427–348 BC) *Republic*

At moments even the grandest aristocrats forgot themselves. Saint-Simon records a memorably shameful instance.

I shall never forget what happened to us at the death of the Prince of Vaudemont's son, by which M. de la Rochefoucauld's family came in for a good inheritance. We were at Marly. The King had been stag-hunting. M. de Chevreuse, whom I found when the King was being unbooted, proposed that we should go and pay our compliments to M. de la Rochefoucauld. We went. Upon entering, what was our surprise, nay, our shame, to find M. de la Rochefoucauld playing at chess with one of his servants in livery, seated opposite to him!

Speech failed us. M. de la Rochefoucauld perceived it, and remained confounded himself. He stammered, he grew confused, he tried to excuse what we had seen, saying that this lackey played very well, and that chessplayers played with everybody. M. de Chevreuse had not come to contradict him, neither had I; we turned the conversation, therefore, and left as soon as possible. As soon as we were outside we opened our minds to each other, and said what we thought of this rare meeting, which, however, we did not make public.

Duc de Saint-Simon, *Memoirs*,
trans. Bayle St. John, 1901

Perhaps the Duke would have given a little less scandal had he acted like a Scottish laird of the late eighteenth century. Walter Scott in the Preface to his novel The Antiquary *(1816) writes of Andrew Gemmells, a professional beggar well known to him in his youth:*

The late Reverend Doctor Robert Douglas, minister of Galashiels, assured the author that the last time he saw Andrew Gemmells, he was engaged in a game at brag with a gentleman of fortune, distinction, and birth. To preserve the due gradations of rank, the party was made at an open window of the château, the laird sitting on his chair in the inside, the beggar on a stool in the yard; and they played on the windowsill.

꩜

In 1815 a play, L'École des Bourgeois, *was acted in Paris. An aristocrat, planning to marry a girl of the middle class, is frustrated when one of his letters is intercepted and read aloud in her family circle:*

'Enfin, mon cher Duc, c'est demain que je m'encanaille' – 'It is tomorrow, my dear Duke, that I join the rabble'.

Dornford Yates, a novelist much obsessed with the aristocracy, once allows a Lady to come to the very edge of the abyss. In the words of Richard Usborne,

When Ann, the Earl's daughter in *And Five were Foolish*, commits the solecism of marrying her father's groom, he takes her to Suet-on-Sea for their honeymoon. He shrivels her up with shame by trying to get trade terms from a Suet cabby ('nothing, it seemed, was to be spared her, nothing'); he lights a cigarette and hands it to her to smoke; and he makes her go on to the pier without a hat. Ann only just survives the horror of it all. Luckily her husband gets killed in a drunken brawl on their wedding night, and Ann can go back to her father's mansion, intact, but a sadder and wiser girl. Suet-on-Sea, the watering place of the lower classes – it's enough to bring any well-born girl to her senses.

Richard Usborne, Clubland Heroes, 1953

It comes as the last nervous echo, in the 1930s, of what had once been a full-throated roar, when in one of the novels of Angela Thirkell the main characters hold an informal meeting to discuss the threat posed to their village by a ruthless developer. The maid in the house asks if the servants, too, can be present; 'Certainly, Jane', is the reply, but as she shuts the door they all roar with laughter. 'No-one could imagine why the servants should want to come to such a meeting.' Perhaps here one detects a certain over-emphasis; the lady doth protest too much.

♔

Next to servants come the hangers-on, the humble friends of the great. Timothy Shy, in exuberant mood, addresses them in a Paean:

SNOBS

Friends of the Rich! whom danger never daunts,
Who tend the Wealthy in their frightful haunts,
Sharing the anguish of their mournful days,
Steadfast to help, to comfort, cheer, and praise –
Stout souls, work on! A silver soup-tureen
Once more has caught Miss Busy on the bean;
Propelled by menial feet through Berkeley Square
Poor Mrs Pegaway has got the air;
In Green Street Mr Freddie's lost his pants,
'Auntie's' been murdered by the rich in Hants,
And Percy, victim of a wild carouse,
Has just been thrown off two more yachts at Cowes.
Miss Upcher's better, though not free from pain,
But Archie Gowle, alas, will never walk again.
They humbly strove; their task was long and grim;
Oft were they playthings of a moneyed whim,
Now welcomed, now expelled with angry shrieks,
Plied with champagne, or gnawed by wayward Pekes.
Be this their guerdon in a glorious cause –
They loved the Rich, whom all the world abhors.

From *Beyond the Headlines*, 1941

Chosen Peoples

No collection of snobs would be complete without a few expressions of national prejudice. Lady Holland tried to discourage Dickens from a projected tour of America in 1845:

Go down to Bristol and see some of the third or fourth class people, and they'll do just as well.

We have a special twist when it is precisely snobbishness of which a nation is accused. Thus in Anthony Powell's novel The Military Philosophers (*1968*) *the narrator is told of the characteristics of the Belgian army:*

They are not, it must be admitted, indifferent to social distinctions. Their assistant Military Attaché, Gauthier de Graef, likes telling a story, no doubt dating from the last war, of an English officer, French officer, and Belgian officer, when a woman rode by on a horse. The Englishman said: 'What a fine horse'; the Frenchman, 'What a fine woman'; the Belgian, 'I wonder what she was née.'

Trollope, himself rather an admirer of American ladies, puts a fine specimen of this feeling into a letter by the foolish Squire Prosper in Mr. Scarborough's Family.

You are about, I am informed, to proceed to the United States, a country against which I entertain a serious antipathy. They are not a gentlemanlike people, and I am given to understand that they are generally dishonest in their dealings. Their President is a low person, and all their ideas of government are pettifogging. Their ladies, I am told, are very vulgar, though I have never had the pleasure of knowing one of them. They are an irreligious nation, and have no respect for the established Church of England and her bishops. I should be very sorry that my heir should go among them . . .

An Oxford don, H. W. Garrod, gave himself the pleasure of finding that Harvard was different from Oxford in being more snobbish:

I hit here an evil which I have no wish to exaggerate. But if I were asked wherein Harvard is least like Oxford, I should feel obliged to say that it is in the sharpness of the social distinctions that it makes, and in the grounds on which those distinctions are based. The social aristocracy of Harvard consists of the men from the private schools. They are a small minority; but they dominate. A man may be a nice man, *and* he may be a good athlete; but unless he has been to a private school it will not help him in the day of social judgement. I had friends in the Harvard football team who came from public schools. The men from the private schools who played in the same team with them did not speak to them in the streets.

H. W. Garrod, *The Study of Good Letters*, 1963

A more serious view of the shortcomings of the nineteenth-century American is found in a letter by the young Henry James, who somehow found in the English the very qualities which Matthew Arnold castigated them for lacking.

Willy asked me in one of his recent letters for an 'opinion of the English', which I haven't yet had time to give – though at times I have felt as if it were a theme in which I could write from a very full mind. In fact, however, I have very little right to have any opinion on the matter. I've seen far too few specimens and those too superficially. The only thing I'm certain about is that I like them – like them heartily. Willy asked me if as individuals they 'kill' the individual American. To this I would say that the Englishmen I have met not only kill, but bury in unfathomable depths, the Americans I have met. A set of people less framed to provoke national self-complacency it would be hard to imagine. There is but one word to use in regard to them – vulgar; vulgar, vulgar. Their ignorance – their stingy, grudging, defiant, attitude towards everything European – their perpetual reference of all things to some American standard or precedent which exists only in their own unscrupulous wind-bags – and then our unhappy poverty of voice, of speech and of physiognomy – these things glare at you hideously. On the other hand, we seem a people of *character*, we seem to have energy, capacity and intellectual stuff in ample measure. What I have pointed at as our vices are the elements of the modern man with *culture* left out. It's the absolute and incredible lack of *culture* that strikes you in common travelling Americans.

Henry James, *Letters*, I, ed. Leon Edel, 1975

One passage in that letter reminds the reader of D. H. Lawrence, and it is only fair to accompany these sneers against America with a typical outburst of Lawrence against England. This one comes from a letter of 3 July 1912, and has a sublime self-comparison.

Curse the blasted, jelly-boned swines, the slimy, the belly-wriggling invertebrates, the miserable sodding rotters, the flaming sods, the snivelling, dribbling, dithering palsied pulseless lot that make up England today . . . Why, why and why was I born an Englishman! – my cursed, rotten-boned, pappy hearted countrymen. Why was I sent to *them*. Christ on the cross must have hated his countrymen. 'Crucify me, you swine', he must have said through his teeth . . .

From S. J. Darroch, *Ottoline*, 1976

It is of course nice to feel superior to one's own countrymen. Cavafy, the modern Alexandrian poet, gives us an amusing example.

'Aristocracy in modern Greece?' *Cavafy once exclaimed.* 'To be an aristocrat there is to have made a corner in coffee in the Peiraeus in 1849.'

Renan felt a comforting contempt for his fellow Frenchmen.

Goncourt describes him watching a crowd which was cheering a regiment on its way to the front, in the Franco-Prussian war.

Renan goes away quickly, with a movement of contempt, saying: 'In all this crowd, there is not one man capable of a noble action!'

But it is also nice to feel superior to other countries. Thus Auden once got into some trouble for saying

I think of Canada as *tiefste Provinz* (the depths of the provinces), where nothing has ever happened and there are no people like me.

Lytton Strachey was pipped by the awfulness of Sweden:

The whole place is too unimaginably bourgeois. I had quite a shock when I entered the dining-room for the first time and saw the crowd of middle-aged and middle-class invalids munching their Swedish cookery. For complete second-rateness this country surpasses the wildest dreams of man. I sometimes fear that it may be the result of democracy, but I imagine really that it's inborn, and brought to its height by lack of cash. All the decent Scandinavians, no doubt, left the place a thousand years ago, and only the dregs remain . . .

Michael Holroyd, *Lytton Strachey: The Unknown Years*, 1967

The Snob in Love

Garrod connected a keen sense of social distinction with the influence of women, and some have gone so far as to ascribe the loss of Britain's empire in India to the coming of the memsahibs in the nineteenth century, who imposed strict barriers of race and class on the original happy-go-lucky attitudes of the eighteenth, when John Company's men rode elephants, kept native mistresses, and lived like the Nabobs they were called. A small book of snobs is not the place to pursue such thoughts very far, but they bring us to that most inflammatory of compounds, the mixture of snobbishness and sex. Love between two people of different classes can be either a comic or a tragic story; when the Prince loves Cinderella, that is conventionally a happy ending, but when Lady Chatterley loves the gamekeeper, we have something different. The range of possibilities is wide. The first piece here, from Daniel Deronda, is an elegantly written example of the familiar pattern of the lady in love with a mere artist; poor Mrs Arrowpoint, who professed egalitarian ideas in her book on Tasso, has the chagrin of finding that her daughter loves her music teacher.

It is hard for us to live up to our own eloquence, and keep pace with our winged words, while we are treading the solid earth and are liable to heavy dining. Besides, it has long been understood that the proprieties of literature are not those of practical life. Mrs Arrowpoint naturally wished for the best of everything. She not only liked to feel herself at a higher level of literary sentiment than the ladies with whom she associated; she wished not to be below them in any point of social consideration. While Klesmer was seen in the light of a patronised musician, his peculiarities were picturesque and acceptable; but to see him by a sudden flash in the light of her son-in-law gave her a burning sense of what the world would say. And the poor lady had been used to represent her Catherine as a model of excellence.

Under the first shock she forgot everything but her anger, and snatched at any phrase that would serve as a weapon.

'If Klesmer has presumed to offer himself to you, your father shall horsewhip him off the premises. Pray, speak, Mr Arrowpoint.'

The father took his cigar from his mouth, and rose to the occasion by saying, 'This will never do, Cath.'

'Do!' cried Mrs Arrowpoint; 'who in their senses ever thought it would do? You might as well say poisoning and strangling will not do. It is a comedy you have got up, Catherine. Else you are mad.'

'I am quite sane and serious, mamma, and Herr Klesmer is not to blame. He never thought of my marrying him. I found out that he loved me, and loving him, I told him I would marry him.'

'Leave that unsaid, Catherine,' said Mrs Arrowpoint, bitterly. 'Every one else will say it for you. You will be a public fable. Every one will say that you must have made the offer to a man who has been paid to come to the house – who is nobody knows what – a gypsy, a Jew, a mere bubble of the earth.'

'Never mind, mamma,' said Catherine, indignant in her turn. 'We all know he is a genius – as Tasso was.'

'Those times were not these, nor is Klesmer Tasso,' said Mrs Arrowpoint, getting more heated. 'There is no sting in *that* sarcasm, except the sting of undutifulness.'

'I am sorry to hurt you, mamma. But I will not give

up the happiness of my life to ideas that I don't believe in and customs I have no respect for.'

'You have lost all sense of duty, then? You have forgotten that you are our only child – that it lies with you to place a great property in the right hands?'

'What are the right hands? My grandfather gained the property in trade.'

'Mr Arrowpoint, *will* you sit by and hear this without speaking?'

'I am a gentleman, Cath. We expect you to marry a gentleman,' said the father, exerting himself.

George Eliot, *Daniel Deronda*, 1876

Another possible attitude to such a difference in rank comes out in Saint-Simon's short obituary of a royal lady; here snobbishness has decidedly the upper hand of love.

Madame de Guise died at this time. Her father was the brother of Louis XIII, and she, humpbacked and deformed to excess, had married the last Duc de Guise, rather than not marry at all. During all their lives, she compelled him to pay her all the deference due to her rank. At table he stood while she unfolded her napkin and seated herself, and did not sit until she told him to do so, and then at the end of the table. This form was observed every day of their lives. She was equally severe in such matters of etiquette with all the rest of the world. She would keep her diocesan, the Bishop of Séez, standing for entire hours, while she was seated in her arm-chair and never once offered him a seat even in the corner.

Memoirs

A grande dame *in a more Wagnerian style is Lady Catherine de Bourgh in* Pride and Prejudice. *We overhear her as she tries to bully the heroine out of an interest in her nephew, Mr Darcy.*

'You are to understand, Miss Bennet, that I came here with the determined resolution of carrying my purpose; nor will I be dissuaded from it. I have not been used to submit to any person's whims. I have not been in the habit of brooking disappointment.'

'*That* will make your ladyship's situation at present more pitiable; but it will have no effect on *me*.'

'I will not be interrupted. Hear me in silence. My daughter and my nephew are formed for each other. They are descended, on the maternal side, from the same noble line; and on the father's, from respectable, honourable, and ancient, though untitled families. Their fortune on both sides is splendid. They are destined for each other by the voice of every member of their respective houses; and what is to divide them? The upstart pretensions of a young woman without family, connections, or fortune. Is this to be endured! But it must not, shall not be. If you were sensible of your own good, you would not wish to quit the sphere in which you have been brought up.'

'In marrying your nephew, I should not consider myself as quitting that sphere. He is a gentleman; I am a gentleman's daughter; so far we are equal.'

'True. You *are* a gentleman's daughter. But who was your mother? Who are your uncles and aunts? Do not imagine me ignorant of their condition.'

'Whatever my connections may be,' said Elizabeth, 'if your nephew does not object to them, they can be nothing to *you*.'

'Tell me once for all, are you engaged to him?'

Though Elizabeth would not, for the mere purpose of obliging Lady Catherine, have answered this question, she could not but say, after a moment's deliberation, 'I am not.'

Lady Catherine seemed pleased.

'And will you promise me, never to enter into such

an engagement?'

'I will make no promise of the kind.'

'Miss Bennet, I am shocked and astonished. I expected to find a more reasonable young woman. But do not deceive yourself into a belief that I will ever recede. I shall not go away, till you have given me the assurance I require.'

'And I certainly *never* shall give it. I am not to be intimidated into anything so wholly unreasonable. Your ladyship wants Mr Darcy to marry your daughter; but would my giving you the wished-for promise, make *their* marriage at all more probable? Supposing him to be attached to me, would *my* refusing to accept his hand, make him wish to bestow it on his cousin? Allow me to say, Lady Catherine, that the arguments with which you have supported this extra-ordinary application, have been as frivolous as the application was ill-judged. You have widely mistaken my character, if you think I can be worked on by such persuasions as these. How far your nephew might approve of your interference in *his* affairs, I cannot tell; but you have certainly no right to concern yourself in mine. I must beg, therefore, to be importuned no farther on the subject.'

'Not so hasty, if you please. I have by no means done. To all the objections I have already urged, I have still another to add. I am no stranger to the particulars of your youngest sister's infamous elopement. I know it all; that the young man's marrying her was a patched-up business, at the expence of your father and uncles. And is *such* a girl to be my nephew's sister? Is *her* husband, is the son of his late father's steward, to be his brother? Heaven and earth! – of what are you thinking? Are the shades of Pemberley to be thus polluted?'

Jane Austen, *Pride and Prejudice*, 1813

Some people find it exciting when a possible partner is above them. Boswell, in Baden-Baden, writes,

The Prince has a particular regard for Madame de Weyfelt; and censorious people go to the length to say that there is love between them. She is not handsome; but the idea of her being a mistress to the Prince made me think of her with a kind of desire . . .

Julien Sorel, the hero of Le Rouge et le Noir, *one of the great sexual snobs of literature, feels not only the simple pleasure of a social inferior who is beloved by a great lady, but also that of having forced her to show emotion while betraying none himself: the triumph of the Stendhalian will. It remains only to add that Stendhal thought him admirable.*

'And so', Julien cried, overcome by sudden passion, 'I, a poor peasant, have had a declaration of love from a great lady!' . . . Then, restraining his delight as much as he could, 'As for me', he went on, 'I have not done badly. I have maintained the dignity of my character. I have never said I loved her . . . ' Another sudden thought struck him, which increased his delight: 'She prefers me to the Marquis de Croisenois!' he cried.

Stendhal, *Le Rouge et le Noir*, 1830

Others find a charm in lowness. We find Flaubert, Sainte-Beuve and Gautier at one in this taste; from the actual records of their dinner conversations in the 1860s Robert Baldick, in his book Dinner at Magny's *(1971), gives us the following dialogue for 8 October 1867.*

'Good for you, Uncle Beuve!' cried Gautier. 'I've always considered that prostitution was the natural state of woman.'

'And an admirable institution as well!' boomed Flaubert. 'If there's one thing I hate in a man – apart from an admiration for Béranger, perfumes, and a fringe beard – it's an aversion to brothels. I've known dozens of worthy young men who had a pious horror of "houses of ill-fame" and yet picked up the loveliest cases of clap you can imagine from their so-called mistresses. It may be a perverse taste, but I love prostitution – and for its own sake, quite apart from what lies beneath. I've never been able to see one of those women in a low-cut dress walking in the rain under the gas-lamps without my heart beating faster, just as the sight of a monk in a robe and a knotted girdle touches some deep ascetic corner of my soul. The idea of prostitution is a meeting point of so many elements – lechery, bitterness, the futility of human relationships, physical frenzy and the clink of gold – that a glance into its depths makes you dizzy and teaches you so much! It makes you so sad, and fills you with such dreams of love!'

'But one can live a full life,' suggested Claudin, 'without frequenting prostitutes.'

'No, you can't!' thundered Flaubert.

It is interesting that George Sand, who was allowed to dine with these thinkers as an honorary man, protested against this doctrine; and that her protest, introducing a breath of humanity into the discussion, was felt to be in such bad taste that she had to leave.

'Men', said Flaubert, 'will always regard sexual pleasure as the most serious thing in life. Because woman, for all the members of my sex, is a Gothic archway opening on to the infinite. That may not be a very high-minded attitude, but it's fundamental to the male.'

'No, I can't accept that,' retorted Sand. 'I'm not a Catholic, but I draw the line at monstrosities. I maintain that old men who buy young girls' bodies aren't making love, and that what they do has nothing in common with Cyprian groves, Gothic arches, the infinite, or males or females. It's something utterly unnatural, because it isn't desire that's pushing the young girl into the old man's arms, and an act in which there's neither liberty nor reciprocity is an offence against the sanctity of Nature . . . '

There was an embarrassed silence, and a slight flush tinged the cheeks of the *bonne dame de Nohant* as she realized that she had gone too far.

'Forgive me, gentlemen,' she said, getting up from her chair. 'I was carried away by my feelings.'

A more sentimental and less brutal variant on this feeling is central to She Stoops to Conquer.

HASTINGS. You have lived pretty much among them. In truth, I have often been surprised, that you who have seen so much of the world, with your natural good sense, and your many opportunities, could never yet acquire a requisite share of assurance.

MARLOW. The Englishman's malady. But tell me, George, where could I have learned that assurance you talk of? My life has been chiefly spent in a college, or an inn, in seclusion from that lovely part of the creation that chiefly teach men confidence. I don't know that I was ever familiarly acquainted with a single modest woman – except my mother – but among females of another class, you know –

HASTINGS. Ay, among them you are impudent enough of all conscience!

MARLOW. They are of *us*, you know.

HASTINGS. But in the company of women of reputation I never saw such an idiot, such a trembler; you look for all the world as if you wanted an opportunity of stealing out of the room.

MARLOW. Why, man, that's because I *do* want to steal out of the room. Faith, I have often formed a resolution to break the ice, and rattle away at any rate. But I don't know how, a single glance from a pair of fine eyes has totally overset my resolution. An impudent fellow may counterfeit modesty, but I'll be hanged if a modest man can ever counterfeit impudence.

HASTINGS. If you could but say half the fine things to them that I have heard you lavish upon the barmaid of an inn, or even a college bedmaker –

MARLOW. Why, George, I can't say fine things to them. They freeze, they petrify me. They may talk of a comet, or a burning mountain, or some such bagatelle. But to me a modest woman, dressed out in all her finery, is the most tremendous object of the whole creation.

Oliver Goldsmith, *She Stoops to Conquer*, 1773

Books of Etiquette had to take account of this low taste in gentlemen, in suitably guarded terms, although of course they did not admit its possibility in ladies. In Manners for Men, *by Mrs Humphry, published in 1897, we read:*

There are young men who make acquaintance with girls in a lower walk of life than their own. It would be an insult to mother or sister to introduce a milliner's apprentice or an assistant from a shop.

These feelings are of course very ancient. Petronius was familiar with both the upward and the downward glance of desire, and combines them in a cynical episode. A maid-servant comes to the hero to tell him that he is loved by a lady.

'As for your confession that you are of humble position, a slave, that adds to the fire of her love. Some women are crazy about what is low, and cannot feel any desire except when they look at a slave or a groom in short clothes . . . My mistress is like that; she skips over the front rows of the theatre and looks for a lover among the crowd at the back.'

My ears full of her seductive words, I asked, 'Please, this lady who loves me – is it really you?'

The maid laughed heartily at this inept question and said 'Don't be so pleased with yourself. I've never gone with a slave – Heaven forbid that I should lavish my love on a gallows-bird. I leave that to the ladies who like to kiss the scars left by the lash. I may be a servant, but I only sit out with gentlemen.'

Petronius Arbiter, Satyricon

A poignant instance of the cruelty of the combination of love and snobbishness is found when the young hero of Great Expectations *first encounters the beautiful and heartless Estella.*

Miss Havisham beckoned her to come close, and took up a jewel from the table, and tried its effect upon her fair young bosom, and against her pretty brown hair. 'Your own, one day, my dear, and you will use it well. Let me see you play cards with this boy.'

'With this boy! Why, he is a common labouring boy!'

I thought I overheard Miss Havisham answer – only it seemed so unlikely – 'Well? You can break his heart.'

'What do you play, boy?' asked Estella of myself with the greatest disdain.

'Nothing but beggar my neighbour, miss.'

'Beggar him,' said Miss Havisham to Estella. So we sat down to cards.

'He calls the knaves Jacks, this boy!' said Estella with disdain, before our first game was out. 'And what coarse hands he has! And what thick boots!'

I had never thought of being ashamed of my hands before; but I began to consider them a very indifferent pair. Her contempt for me was so strong, that it became infectious, and I caught it.

She won the game, and I dealt. I misdealt, as was only natural, when I knew she was lying in wait for me to do wrong; and she denounced me for a stupid, clumsy labouring boy.

Charles Dickens, *Great Expectations*, 1861

Two comic variations follow. In Firbank's novel The
Flower Beneath the Foot *(1923), Prince Yousef of
Pisuerga is enamoured of a maid of honour, whom we find
in this scene reading to the Queen.*

'Give me my diamond anemones,' the Queen com-
manded, and motioning to her Maid: 'Pray conclude,
mademoiselle, those lofty lines.'

With a slight sigh, the lectress took up the posture
of a Dying Intellectual . . .

'Live with an aim, and let that aim be high!' she
reiterated in tones tinged perceptibly with emotion.

'But not *too* high, remember, Mademoiselle de
Nazianzi . . . '

There was a short pause. And then –

'Ah, Madam! What a dearest he is!'

'I think you forget yourself,' the Queen murmured
with a quelling glance. 'You had better withdraw.'

'He has such strength! One could niche an idol in
his dear, dinted chin.'

'Enough!'

And a moment later the enflamed girl left the room
warbling softly: *Depuis le Jour.*

'Holy Virgin,' the Countess said, addressing herself
to the ceiling. 'Should his Weariness, the Prince, yield
himself to this caprice . . . '

The Queen shifted a diamond bangle from one of
her arms to the other.

'She reads at such a pace,' she complained, 'and when
I asked her *where* she had learnt to read so quickly,
she replied "On the screens at Cinemas." '

'I do not consider her at all distinguished,' the
Countess commented, turning her eyes away towards
the room.

Later the Queen remonstrates with her son:

'But what can you *see* in her?' his mother mourned.
'She suits my feelings', the Prince simply said.
'Peuh!'
'She meets my needs.'
'She's so housemaid . . . I hardly know!' The Queen raised beautiful hands, bewildered.
'Très gutter, ma'am', the Countess murmured, dropping her voice to a half-whisper.
'She saves us from cliché', the Prince indignantly said.

Evelyn Waugh put an unexpected aspect of the subject on sound snobbish lines when he wrote,

Impotence and sodomy are socially O.K., but birth control is flagrantly middle-class.

It is a nice example of the combination of sex and snobbishness that the Marquis de Boissy, who married Byron's last mistress Teresa Guiccioli, took pride in her affair with the poet. One story told that when a French Peer asked him, cautiously, whether his fiancée were related to the Countess Guiccioli whose name had been connected with Byron's, he replied, with a radiant smile, 'Comment donc! Mais c'est elle-même, c'est elle!' Another version said that he introduced her as 'Ma femme, ancienne maîtresse de Byron'.

The clash of class and sex can be a subject of the most serious poetry. The brothers of the Duchess of Malfi are enraged by her marriage to

A slave that only smelled of ink and counters,
And never in's life looked like a gentleman.

John Webster, *The Duchess of Malfi, c.* 1614

The brothers of Lorenzo, the beloved of Keats's Isabella, were

> well nigh mad
> That he, the servant of their trade designs,
> Should in their sister's love be blithe and glad.
>
> *Isabella, or the Pot of Basil,* 1820

In both of these cases the result was tragedy. In Tennyson's Idylls of the King the lady Lynette treats the knight Gareth, whom she thinks to be a kitchen boy, with disdain.

> What does thou, scullion, in my fellowship?
> Dish-washer and broach-turner, loon! to me
> Thou smellest all of kitchen as before . . .

In the end Lynette is made to eat her words. In the original version of the story Gareth married her sister; but a later sensibility preferred to make the knight fall in love with the haughty lady herself.

Stendhal, who devoted much thought to the interaction of sex and snobbishness, gives a sour analysis of matters in England.

It appears to me that an English husband's pride skilfully inflames his poor wife's vanity. It convinces her above all that she must not be *vulgar*, and mothers who are preparing their daughters to find husbands have grasped this idea very clearly. That is why *fashion* is much more absurd and more tyrannical in hard-headed England than in the bosom of light-hearted France; it is in Bond Street that the *carefully careless* was conceived. In England fashion is a duty, in Paris it is a pleasure. Fashion erects a much stouter brazen wall in London between New Bond Street and Fenchurch Street than it does in Paris between the Chaussée d'Antin and the Rue Saint-Martin. Husbands willingly allow their wives this aristocratic folly in compensation for the enormous amount of sadness they inflict on them. An excellent picture of women's life in England as it has been moulded by the taciturn pride of Englishmen, is, I think, to be found in the once famous novels of Miss Burney. Since to ask for a glass of water when one is thirsty is vulgar, Miss Burney's heroines do not fail to let themselves die of thirst. In trying to avoid vulgarity one arrives at the most abominable affectation.

Stendhal on Love, trans. H.B.V., 1927

Another form of snobbishness is the feeling of superiority which one sex can feel towards the other, a common thing in the young. Cyril Connolly's youthful letters to Noel Blakiston, now published as A Romantic Friendship *(1975), give a rather precious example. Here he writes from Jamaica.*

Girls are important in a country where no man has been educated enough to be individual, because they at least are decorative and gentle. To love them on the other hand seems to me unthinkable they are so ungainly and so ordinary besides which the whole business of flirtation, the triteness of passion, the dreariness of marriage seem altogether disgusting. Also their influence on men is for the worse, they encourage 'manliness', vanity and worldly ambitions and they reduce all male beauty to a question of height and uniform – and they are so dull. Friendship with them is possible and advantageous in a place like this but anywhere else entirely unnecessary . . . Male loves at least bear fruit in masterpieces like gravel in an oyster.

God & the Snob

The other most potent thing to combine with snobbishness is of course religion. Again the mixture can take many forms. Chamfort records that 'M. de Brissac, intoxicated with gentility, often referred to God with the phrase "The Gentleman on high"'; and Saint-Simon gives us another exquisitely artless glimpse of the pride of the ancien régime.

About this time died the Maréchale de la Meilleray, aged eighty-eight. She was the paternal aunt of the Maréchal de Villeroy and the Duc de Brissac, his brother-in-law. It was she who unwittingly put that cap on MM. de Brissac, which they have ever since worn in their arms, and which has been imitated. She was walking in a picture gallery of her ancestors one day with her niece, a lively, merry person, whom she obliged to salute and be polite to each portrait, and who in pleasant revenge persuaded her that one of the said portraits wore a cap which proved him to be an Italian Prince. She swallowed this, and had the cap introduced into her arms, despite her family, who are now obliged to keep it, but who always call it, 'My Aunt's cap.' On another occasion, people were speaking in her presence of the death of the Chevalier de Savoie, brother of the Comte de Soissons and of the famous Prince Eugène, who died very young, very suddenly, very debauched, and full of benefices. The talk became religious. She listened some time, and then, with a profound look of conviction, said: 'For my part, I am persuaded that God will think twice about damning a man of such high birth as that!' This caused a burst of laughter, but nothing could make her change her opinion.

Memoirs

Knightly Chetwood (1650–1720), Dean of Gloucester, achieved celebrity when, preaching at Court, he threatened sinners with punishment in 'a place which he thought it not decent to name in so polite an assembly.'

Among the Methodists, Selina, Countess of Huntingdon, was treated with a reverence which had its comical side. Ronald Knox in his book Enthusiasm *(1950) deals with the biography of her Ladyship which was written by 'A Member of the Houses of Shirley and Hastings.'*

The book is in fact a monument of pietism, and pietism disfigured by unremitting snobbishness. 'Those Peeresses who had found, at the Cross and Mercy-seat, the happiness they had sought in vain from the world', 'Mrs Deane was considered as ranking among the higher circles' – a hundred such expressions arrest and exasperate the reader; nor does he take more kindly to the sisters-in-law of his heroine when he is told that they 'were amiably condescending to all their inferiors, even the poorest', and that 'under the ministry of Mr Ingham, the Lord met these exalted females with all the blessings of his grace'. Ceremonious forms of address are so strictly observed that you may easily miss the subtle flavour of such a phrase as 'his Lordship was condemned to be hanged'. All this is the more regrettable, because the stalwarts of the Evangelical Movement, somewhat dazzled by the high society their hostess introduced them to, were apt to speak of her, write to her, in terms not far removed from flunkeyism. It is on record – Whitefield himself is our authority – that when Lady Huntingdon was ill and prayers were offered at the Tabernacle for her recovery, thousands joined in singing the following verses for her Ladyship:

> Gladly we join to pray for those
> Who, rich with worldly honours, shine,
> Who dare to own a Saviour's cause,
> And in that hated cause to join:
> Yes, we would praise thee that a few
> Love thee, though rich and noble too.

> Uphold this star in thy right hand –
> Crown her endeavours with success;
> Among the great ones may she stand,
> A witness of thy righteousness,
> Till many nobles join thy train
> And triumph in the Lamb that's slain.

A pious aristocrat might have a mixture of feelings about a priest. Here the hero of Le Rouge et le Noir *is being instructed about the position he will occupy as a secretary who is also a seminarist, in a noble household.*

'We are priests', added M. Pirard, 'for Mme. de la Mole will take you for one. She thinks of priests as a sort of upper servant, indispensable for her salvation.'

'It seems to me,' Julien replied, 'that I shall not be staying very long in Paris.'

Saki gives us a lady who patronizes God himself.

'That', said the Princess, 'is a portrait of the old Princess Lorikoff. She lived in Millionaya Street, near the Winter Palace, and was one of the Court ladies of the Old Russian school. Her knowledge of people and events was extremely limited; but she used to patronize everyone who came into contact with her. There was a story that when she died and left the Millionaya for Heaven she addressed St. Peter in her formal staccato French: "Je suis la Princesse Lor-i-koff. Il me donne grand plaisir de faire votre connaissance. Je vous en prie de me présenter au Bon Dieu." St. Peter made the desired introduction, and the Princess addressed le Bon Dieu: "Je suis la Princesse Lor-i-koff. Il me donne grand plaisir à faire votre connaissance. On a souvent parlé de vous à l'église de la rue Million." '

Saki (H. H. Munro), *Reginald in Russia*, 1910

From the point of view of aesthetic rather than social snobbishness the story was told of Charles Eliot Norton, the great Harvard aesthete, that when he got to Heaven he cried, 'Oh, oh! so overdone! so Renaissance!'

👑

But some of the doctrines of religion can themselves be made to wear a snobbish appearance. An anonymous poet writes of Predestination:

> We are the precious chosen few;
>   The rest will all be damned.
> There isn't room in Heaven for you –
>   We can't have Heaven crammed.

The charm of the following extract, which comes from the notes made by Lord Stanhope of his conversations with the Duke of Wellington, is the belief of the writer that he is truly acting out the commandments of his religion.

After dinner the Duke spoke *inter alia* of church accommodation and extension, condemning the whole system of pews. He said that if space were wanted in Strathfieldsaye he should certainly offer to give up his pew, retaining only a chair for himself. 'The system of a church establishment is,' added he, 'that every clergyman should preach the word of God, and that every parishioner should be able to hear the word of God. Is it not then quite contrary to that system, that by means of handsome family pews twenty or thirty persons of rank should take up the space of two or three hundred?'

I most cordially concurred in this opinion, which I have long entertained. A church appears to me the very last place where any distinction of rank should prevail, or any sentiment of pride be indulged. I should think it far more consistent with the feelings that make one enter a church at all, to kneel side by side with those whom I should keep at a distance elsewhere – by the side of my own footman or my own cobbler.

Certainly, the Roman Catholics manage this point far better than we do.

And a lady in Firbank's Inclinations *goes even further. 'After all', she enquired, 'isn't heaven a sort of snobbishness? A looking-up, a preference for the best hotel?'*

But the last word shall go to the Duc de Saint-Simon. He tells with indignation of an intolerable affront given to the Dukes by the Princes of the Blood. When the

King attended communion at Versailles, the two senior Dukes removed the altar cloth. But by a trick the Princes of the Blood managed to deprive them of this right and confine it to themselves. The King, despite passionate complaints, refused to intervene, and Saint-Simon concludes his indignant account by saying 'never, since that time, did I go to the communion of the King.' Such were the forms into which snobbishness could force the religion of humility . . .

Inverted Snobbery

The times we live in are at least as prone to inverted snobbishness as to the straightforward article. That too, of course, is nothing new; Josiah Bounderby of Coke Town, in Hard Times, *pretends to be the lowest of the low, the son of a nameless slut, brought up in the gutter, and is much mortified when suddenly his respectable and devoted mother is brought forward. Sir Osbert Sitwell tells of the horrors of his first day at school, and we see the poor boy trapped between the inverted snobbishness of his contemporaries and the true snobbishness of his mother.*

I had no time to examine the yard, or indeed anything but the jostling, screaming mob that occupied it, for it teemed with shouting, whistling, roaring schoolboys of different ages and sizes ... I looked around and felt rather out of it – but not for long. Evidently I had been expected, for about half the larger boys, directly they saw me, set upon me with whirling fists and yells of 'Don't think you're everybody just because your father's a bloody baronet!' Now this was, as a matter of fact, something which had not occurred to me heretofore, because my mother made no secret of her view that a baronetcy was a disgrace and that she regarded baronets in general as the Ishmaels of the British race; and no one else had ever mentioned it to me. None the less, I returned from my first encounter with victorious British democracy suffering from two black eyes, an aching body, and sore heart.

Left Hand, Right Hand, 1946

*More recently a journalist described seeing a young man
kicking a car. When a passing pedestrian remonstrated,
he replied, 'It's a Rolls, innit?'*

👑

*At the extreme, this attitude becomes that which Tom
Wolfe has named Radical Chic. From his book of that
title comes the following passage on servants: how, as a
progressive person of great wealth, is one to entertain
those of the deprived who are in fashion, without social
awkwardness about the servants? (And one must have
servants).*

After a while, it all comes down to servants. They are
the cutting edge in Radical Chic. Obviously, if you are
giving a party for the Black Panthers, as Lenny and
Felicia Bernstein are this evening, or as Sidney and
Gail Lumet did last week, or as John Simon of Random
House and Richard Baron, the publisher, did before
that; or for the Chicago Eight, such as the party Jean
van den Heuvel gave; or for the grape workers or
Bernadette Devlin, such as the parties Andrew Stein
gave; or for the Young Lords, such as the party Ellie
Guggenheimer is giving next week in *her* Park Avenue
duplex; or for the Indians or the SDS or the G.I.
coffee shops or even for the Friends of the Earth – well,
then, obviously you can't have a Negro butler and
maid, Claude and Maude, in uniform, circulating
through the living room, the library, and the main hall
serving drinks and canapés. Plenty of people have tried
to think it out. They try to picture the Panthers or
whoever walking in bristling with electric hair and
Cuban shades and leather pieces and the rest of it, and
they try to picture Claude and Maude with the black
uniforms coming up and saying, 'Would you care for
a drink, sir?' They close their eyes and try to picture
it *some way*, but there *is* no way. One simply cannot

see that moment. So the current wave of Radical Chic has touched off the most desperate search for white servants.

Mr Tony Benn (né Wedgwood Benn), with his celebrated entries in Who's Who, *gives us a guide to the progress of this sort of inverted snobbery. In 1969 his entry told the world that he was 'Ed.: Westminster School; New Coll. Oxford.' In 1975 this had changed to 'Ed.: still in progress.' And in 1979 he did not appear in* Who's Who *at all ...*

♛

George Orwell, taking a friend into a pub, asked him what he would have. 'Oh, a glass of beer', was the reply. Orwell asked the barmaid for 'A pint of bitter, and a glass of beer for my friend.' To his remonstrance that 'You didn't have to say that', Orwell replied 'Did you ever hear a working man ask for "a glass of beer"? 'But I'm not a working man', answered the friend. 'Well, you needn't boast of it', was Orwell's crushing retort.

Wider Yet & Wider

It would be a shame to end this book on a note almost serious. Let it close rather with a few final squibs, to show that there is nothing which cannot be thought of in snobbish terms. First, the flowers are imagined, by Firbank, as speaking in a flower shop.

And in the little closed shop behind the heavy moucharaby now that they had all gone, the exhalations of the *flowers* arose; pungent, concerted odours, expressive of natural antipathies and feuds, suave alliances, suffering, pride, and joy.... Only the shining moon through the moucharaby, illumining here a lily, there a leaf, may have guessed what they were saying:

'My wires are hurting me: my wires are hurting me.'

'I have no water. I cannot reach the water.'

'They have pushed me head down into the bottom of the bowl.'

'I'm glad I'm in a Basket! No one will hurl *me* from a window to be bruised underfoot by the callous crowd.'

'It's uncomfy, isn't it, without one's roots?'

'You Weed you! You, you, you . . . *buttercup*! How dare you, to *an Orchid*!'

'I shouldn't object to sharing the same water with him, dear . . . ordinary as he is! If *only* he wouldn't smell. . . . '

'She's nothing but a piece of common grass, and so I tell her!'

Upon the tense pent atmosphere surged a breath of

cooler air, and through the street-door slipped the Duchess of Varna . . .

The Flower Beneath the Foot, 1923

A private advertisement in The Times:

Sports car, preferably foreign, wanted week-end 22 June by respectable middle-aged civil servant, to raise son's status at preparatory school where most fathers have Jaguars.

A shopkeeper can feel proud of his lack of success. A paragraph from the Evening Standard:

Amid all this commercial cheer Gieves of Bond Street struck a dignified but sombre note. They are not doing so well with their shirts this Christmas. 'We have heard of the bonanzas enjoyed by some of the big stores. Our customers are probably more susceptible to government policies – they tend to have their money in the City, you know; whereas the Oxford Street type of shopper keeps it in a jar on the mantelpiece.'

But success can make him no less haughty, as Tom Brown observes in his Laconics (*1701*):

Well, this thing call'd Prosperity makes a man strangely insolent and forgetful. How contemptibly a Cutler looks at a poor Grinder of Knives, a Physician in his Coach at a Farrier a Foot, and a well-grown *Pauls Churchyard* Bookseller upon one of the Trade that sells Secondhand Books under the Trees, in *Morefields*.

Beachcomber's archetypal boarding-house keeper, Mrs McGurgle, gives us a glimpse of the social hierarchy of the seaside holiday.

MRS MCGURGLE AGAIN

Dear Sir,

I can well imagine what the late Mr McGurgle – him that I have said fell a victim to tainted Continental cocoa and should have known better than to tempt fate by ordering it so far from home – would have had to say of a proprietress who graded her helpings according to the birth and education of the clientèle. Why, I remember once it was our privilege to receive as a paying guest at Marine House a very high official of the gas company. It is true we gave him a big room, him having so much luggage, but when it came to meal-times, I can hear my late husband saying, as though it was yesterday, 'Flo, put the gentleman between the insurance clerk and the piano-tuner. He is only one of us while he enjoys the shelter of the McGurgle roof.' And I flatter myself that when I stood up to help the gravy, gas company or no gas company, his portion did not outweigh that of his neighbours, nor was the smile I directed to the least of our patrons, Miss Ansper, the orphan of a night-watchman whom diphtheria and complications carried to a premature burial in the northern corner of St. Oswith's cemetery, any less friendly than that reserved for the official who, be it added, for all his luggage and fine airs, knew no better than to stove his morning egg in at a blow with his thumb.

> Yours truly,
> Florence McGurgle
>
> From *The Best of Beachcomber*,
> ed. Michael Frayn, 1963

I have said little of class-distinction in vocabulary, a subject so well ventilated by Nancy Mitford. Here is an old example, in which, about 1800, a Scottish lady prides herself on avoiding a damning word.

Thus one Scotticism was held in terror by those who used a different Scotticism: as at Inveraray, the wife of the chief writer of the place, seeking to secure her guest from the taint of inferior society, intimated to him, but somewhat confidentially, that Mrs W— (the rival writer's wife) was quite a vulgar body, so much so as to ask any one leaving the room to '*snib* the door', instead of bidding them, as she triumphantly observed, '*sneck* the door'.

Even illness can have its class distinctions. The idea of a 'distinguished stoop' is familiar, and the implications of 'rude health' are clear. P. G. Wodehouse, in Eggs, Beans, and Crumpets *(1951), constructs a hierarchy of illness. Freddie Fitch-Fitch is trying to induce his uncle, who is resident at Droitwich Spa for his gout, to sign the papers releasing his capital, so that he can get married.*

'Uncle,' he said, 'may I trouble you for a moment? . . . These papers.'

Sir Aylmer cocked an eye at the documents.

'What papers are those?'

'The ones you have to sign, releasing my capital.'

'Oh, those,' said Sir Aylmer genially. The music had plainly mellowed him. 'Of course, yes. Certainly, certainly. Give me . . . '

He broke off, and Freddie saw that he was looking at a distinguished, silvery-haired man with thin, refined features, who was sauntering by.

'Afternoon, Rumbelow,' he said.

There was an unmistakable note of obsequiousness in Sir Aylmer's voice. His face had become pink, and he was shuffling his feet and twiddling his fingers. The man to whom he had spoken paused and looked down. Seeing who it was that accosted him, he raised a silvery eyebrow. His manner was undisguisedly supercilious.

'Ah, Bastable,' he said distantly.

A duller man than Sir Aylmer Bastable could not have failed to detect the cold hauteur in his voice. Freddie saw the flush on his uncle's face deepen. Sir Aylmer mumbled something about hoping that the distinguished-looking man was feeling better today.

'Worse,' replied the other curtly, 'Much worse. The doctors are baffled. Mine is a very complicated case.' He paused for a moment, and his delicately chiselled lip curled in a sneer. 'And how is the gout, Bastable? Gout! Ha, ha!'

Without waiting for a reply he passed on and joined a group that stood chatting close by. Sir Aylmer choked down a mortified oath.

'Snob!' he muttered. 'Thinks he's everybody just because he's got telangiectasis. I don't see what's so wonderful about having telangiectasis. Anybody could have . . . What on earth are you doing? What the devil's all this you're waving under my nose? Papers? Papers? I don't want any papers. Take them away, sir!'

Finally, even a family ghost can become an object of dread, not supernatural but social. O. Henry's story A Ghost of a Chance *turns on this point, beginning:*

'Actually, a *hod*!' repeated Mrs Kinsolving, pathetically.

Mrs Bellmore arched a sympathetic eyebrow. Thus she expressed condolence and a generous amount of apparent surprise.

'Fancy her telling everywhere', recapitulated Mrs Kinsolving, 'that she saw a ghost in the apartment she occupied here – our choicest guest-room – a ghost, carrying a hod on its shoulder – the ghost of an old man in overalls, smoking a pipe and carrying a hod! The very absurdity of the thing shows her malicious intent. There never was a Kinsolving that carried a hod . . . '

👑

Snobbishness does not rest, even in the grave, but I must allow my readers to rest from its study. Dr Johnson, who always had the last word, shall be allowed to have it here, too; and an Oxford don reminds himself that when he said it, he was speaking of the passions of scholars. 'Small things make mean men proud,' said Johnson, 'and vanity catches small occasions.' And, there perhaps, we can leave it.

Acknowledgements

The editor and publishers gratefully acknowledge permission to use copyright material in this book:

Daisy Ashford: From *The Young Visiters* (1919). Reprinted by permission of the Author's Literary Estate and Chatto & Windus Ltd.

Robert Baldick: From *Dinner at Magny's* (Gollancz, 1971/ Coward McCann 1972). Copyright © 1971, 1972 by Robert Baldick. Reprinted by permission of Anthony Sheil Associates Ltd., and Julian Bach Literary Agency, Inc.

Max Beerbohm: From *Zuleika Dobson* (1911). Reprinted by permission of William Heinemann Ltd.

Hilaire Belloc: 'Godolphin Horne' from *Cautionary Tales for Children* (1907). Reprinted by permission of Gerald Duckworth & Co. Ltd.

John Betjeman: From 'Beside the Seaside' from *Collected Poems* (Murray, 1970/Houghton Mifflin, 1971). Reprinted by permission of John Murray (Publishers) Ltd.

Sir Henry Channon: From *The Diaries of Sir Henry ('Chips') Channon*, edited by Robert Rhodes James, 1967. Reprinted by permission of Weidenfeld & Nicolson.

N. C. Chaudhuri: From *Scholar Extraordinary* (1974). Reprinted by permission of the author and Chatto & Windus Ltd.

Cyril Connolly: From *A Romantic Friendship* (1975). Reprinted by permission of Constable Publishers.

Scott Fitzgerald: Extract from 'The Rich Boy' from *The Bodley Head Scott Fitzgerald*, Vol. V, and also in *All The Sad Young Men*. Copyright 1926 Charles Scribner's Sons; copyright renewed. Reprinted by permission of The Bodley Head, and Charles Scribner's Sons.

David Garnett: From *The Golden Echo* (1953). Reprinted by permission of the Author's Literary Estate and Chatto & Windus Ltd.

H. W. Garrod: From *The Study of Good Letters*, edited by John Jones, p. 184. © Oxford University Press 1963. Reprinted by permission of Oxford University Press.

Robert Halsband: From *The Life of Lady Mary Wortley Montague* (1956), pp. 255–6. Reprinted by permission of Oxford University Press.

ACKNOWLEDGEMENTS

T. F. Higham: From *Dr Blakiston Recalled* (1967). Reprinted by permission of Basil Blackwell Publisher.

Michael Holroyd: Extracts from *Lytton Strachey* (1967). Reprinted by permission of William Heinemann Ltd.

Aldous Huxley: From *Crome Yellow* (1921). Reprinted by permission of Mrs Laura Huxley, Chatto & Windus Ltd., and Harper & Row, Inc.

Henry James: Extract from a letter to Mrs Henry James Sr. from Florence Hôtel de l'Europe dated 13 October 1869. Published in *The Letters of Henry James*, Vol. I, 1843–1875 (Harvard, 1974/Macmillan, 1975).

Ronald Knox: Extract (and 2 verses quoted from *Lady Huntingdon's Life*, 1840, vol. 1) from *Enthusiasm* (1950), pp. 484–5. Reprinted by permission of Oxford University Press.

D. H. Lawrence: From a previously unpublished letter which first appeared in *Ottoline* (S. J. Darroch, Chatto, 1976). Reprinted by permission of Laurence Pollinger Ltd., and the Estate of the late Mrs Frieda Lawrence Ravagli.

Anita Loos: From *Gentlemen Prefer Blondes*. Copyright © 1925, by The International Magazine Co., Inc. (*Harper's Bazaar*). Copyright © 1925 by Anita Loos. Copyright © R. 1953, by Anita Loos Emerson. Copyright © 1963 by Anita Loos. Reprinted by permission of Liveright Publishing Corp.

Elsa Maxwell: From *I Married the World* (1955). Reprinted by permission of William Heinemann Ltd., and Little, Brown & Company.

Diana Morgan: 'Kensington Girls' from *My Sex, Right or Wrong* (Methuen).

J. B. Morton: From *The Best of Beachcomber*, edited by Michael Frayn (Heinemann, 1963). Reprinted by permission of A. D. Peters Ltd.

Myles na Gopaleen: From *The Best of Myles* (1968). Reprinted by permission of Granada Publishing Ltd., and A. M. Heath Ltd. for the Estate of the late Flann O'Brien.

Harold Nicolson: From *Some People* (1927). Reprinted by permission of Constable Publishers and Nigel Nicolson, Literary Executor to Harold Nicolson.

Ezra Pound: From 'The Prose Tradition in Verse' from *Literary Essays of Ezra Pound*. Copyright © 1935 by Ezra Pound. Reprinted by permission of Faber & Faber Ltd., and New Directions Publ. Corp., New York.

Anthony Powell: From *The Military Philosophers* (1958). Reprinted by permission of William Heinemann Ltd., and David Higham Associates Ltd.

Marcel Proust: From *Remembrance of Things Past*, Vol. 2, pp. 443–4 and pp. 973–4 in the translation by C. K. Scott-Moncrieff and Terence Kilmartin. Copyright © 1981 by

Random House, Inc. and Chatto & Windus Ltd. Reprinted by permission of Chatto & Windus Ltd., and Random House, Inc.

Justin Richardson: Extract from the poem 'Titles', first published in *Punch*, 11 April 1951. Reproduced by permission of *Punch*.

Timothy Shy: From *Beyond the Headlines* (Penguin Books, 1941), pp. 53–4. Copyright © Timothy Shy, 1941. Reprinted by permission of Penguin Books Ltd.

Sir Osbert Sitwell: From *Left Hand, Right Hand* (Macmillan, 1946). Reprinted by permission of David Higham Associates Ltd.

Richard Usborne: From *Clubland Heroes* (1953). Reprinted by permission of Constable Publishers.

Auberon Waugh: From *The Foxglove Saga*. Copyright © 1961 by Auberon Waugh. Reprinted by permission of Associated Book Publishers Ltd., and Literistic Ltd.

Evelyn Waugh: From *A Little Learning* (Chapman & Hall). Reprinted by permission of A. D. Peters & Co. Ltd.

P. G. Wodehouse: Extracts from *Uncle Fred in the Springtime* (1939) and *Eggs, Beans and Crumpets* (1940). Reprinted by permission of A. P. Watt Ltd. for the Estate of P. G. Wodehouse and The Hutchinson Group Ltd., and Scott Meredith Literary Agency, Inc., New York.

Tom Wolfe: From *Radical Chic & Mau-Mauing the Flak Catchers*. Copyright © 1970 by Tom Wolfe. Reprinted by permission of Farrar, Straus and Giroux, Inc., and International Creative Management, New York.

Virginia Woolf: From 'A Change of Perspective', Vol. 3 of the *Letters of Virginia Woolf*, edited by Nigel Nicolson and Joanne Trautmann (pp. 188 and 146 of the Hogarth Press edition). Reprinted by permission of The Hogarth Press for the Author's Literary Estate, and Harcourt Brace Jovanovich, Inc.

While every effort has been made to secure permission, we may have failed in a few cases to trace the copyright holder. We apologize for any apparent negligence.

The illustrations in this book were taken from the following sources; H. W. Caslon & Co. Ltd., *Types, Borders, & Initials* (London, 1930); Clarence P. Hornung, *Handbook of Early Advertising Art* (New York, 1956); Irving Zucker, *A Source Book of French Advertising Art* (London, 1970).

Index